T0304038

ROUTLEDGE LIBRARY EDITIONS:
TAXATION

Volume 9

TAXATION IN CENTRALLY PLANNED ECONOMIES

TAXATION IN CENTRALLY PLANNED ECONOMIES

P.T. WANLESS

LONDON AND NEW YORK

First published in 1985 by Croom Helm Ltd

This edition first published in 2019
by Routledge
2 Park Square, Milton Park, Abingdon, Oxon OX14 4RN

and by Routledge
711 Third Avenue, New York, NY 10017

Routledge is an imprint of the Taylor & Francis Group, an informa business

© 1985 P.T. Wanless

All rights reserved. No part of this book may be reprinted or reproduced or utilised in any form or by any electronic, mechanical, or other means, now known or hereafter invented, including photocopying and recording, or in any information storage or retrieval system, without permission in writing from the publishers.

Trademark notice: Product or corporate names may be trademarks or registered trademarks, and are used only for identification and explanation without intent to infringe.

British Library Cataloguing in Publication Data
A catalogue record for this book is available from the British Library

ISBN: 978-1-138-56291-2 (Set)
ISBN: 978-0-429-48988-4 (Set) (ebk)
ISBN: 978-0-8153-4969-3 (Volume 9) (hbk)
ISBN: 978-1-351-10721-1 (Volume 9) (ebk)

Publisher's Note
The publisher has gone to great lengths to ensure the quality of this reprint but points out that some imperfections in the original copies may be apparent.

Disclaimer
The publisher has made every effort to trace copyright holders and would welcome correspondence from those they have been unable to trace.

TAXATION IN CENTRALLY PLANNED ECONOMIES

P. T. Wanless

CROOM HELM
London & Sydney

©1985 P.T. Wanless
Croom Helm Ltd, Provident House, Burrell Row,
Beckenham, Kent BR3 1AT

Croom Helm Australia Pty Ltd, Suite 4, 6th Floor,
64-76 Kippax Street, Surry Hills, NSW 2010, Australia

British Library Cataloguing in Publication Data

Wanless, P.T.
Taxation in centrally planned economics.
1. Taxation 2. Central planning
I. Title
330.12'4 HJ2305

ISBN 0-7099-3639-7

Printed and bound in Great Britain by
Biddles Ltd, Guildford and King's Lynn

CONTENTS

LIST OF TABLES

ACKNOWLEDGEMENTS

In all my work I owe an enormous debt of gratitude to the late Dr Janusz G. Zielinski of the Institute of Soviet and East European Studies, University of Glasgow, who first guided and inspired me in my researches on the socialist economy. I am also grateful to many Polish economists who assisted me in study trips to Poland, especially Professor Z. Fedorowicz and Dr Barbara Kolonowska-Kowalska.

In writing this particular book, I would like to express particular thanks to Dr P. G. Hare, Department of Economics, University of Stirling; to Dr R. A. Clarke of the Institute of Soviet and East European Studies, University of Glasgow; and to Dr A. Young and Mr A. Galloway, Department of Economics and Management, Paisley College of Technology. Further thanks are due to Dr Stephen Barr, Editor, Cambridge University Press, Mr Peter Sowden, Editor, Croom Helm, Publishers, and to various anonymous publisher's readers; I would like to thank them for their thorough and constructive comments which were of great assistance to me.

Finally, I am grateful to the secretarial staff of the Department of Economics and Management at Paisley College, for their patience in deciphering the manuscript, for typing and retyping subsequent drafts. Mrs Robertson, of Aid-U Staff Services Agency, Glasgow, typed the final camera-ready copy, and I would like to thank her for an accurate and high quality piece of work.

None of the above have any responsibility for any remaining mistakes, or lack of clarity in the book. Any such faults are definitely my own.

This book is dedicated to my husband, Eric Harvie, and to my sons, Christopher J. L. Harvie and Vincent J. O. Harvie, who have so unselfishly organised their lives so that I have had time to write this book.

INTRODUCTION

OBJECTIVES

The origins of this book were found in my researches for my PhD thesis 'Economic Policy and Taxation in Poland in the 1970's' (University of Strathclyde, 1982). In the course of that study, I found there was a general dearth of literature in English which dealt with the role of taxation and the State Budget in a centrally planned economy. Such studies as there were tended to deal with case studies of particular countries, and there appeared to be no general work which dealt with the theory of taxation in a centrally planned economy. There was, I felt, a need for a work which would explain the rationale for the existence of a State Budget, and for the taxes which a socialist government imposed on socially owned industry, and would explain the relationship between the budgetary mechanism and the central planning mechanism. Without such a general perspective on the socialist State Budget, empirical studies (like my PhD thesis) would tend to be highly specialised, very descriptive, and, to some extent, lacking in theoretical content. Theoretical perspectives on socialist taxation in my PhD thesis were partly applications of conventional public finance theory, suitably adapted by me; or incorporated ideas, which were to be found in the few specialised works which dealt at all with taxation and the State Budget in a centrally planned economy; or were taken from a more extensive Polish literature, not generally available to non-Polish speakers. There was, I felt, a need to take these ideas out of the context of an historical and descriptive study of Polish experience, and try and generalise them to apply to 'socialist' (centrally planned) economies in general.

This approach led me on to consider the diversity of economic institutions and economic management systems in centrally planned economies. It had become obvious to me that the Polish economic reforms had altered the qualitative importance of taxation and the State Budget, had altered the economic objectives which taxation was intended to achieve, and had led to the introduction of new types of taxes. There was, I felt, a substantial difference between the role of taxation in a 'command' economy, and its role in economic reforms. This difference had to be incorporated into my general perspective on the role of taxation in a socialist economy.

Thus I found there were two themes in my planned book: the economics of socialist taxation, and the economics of socialist economic reform. To embrace both of these themes, I found that I needed a theory of the role of the State, which would encompass both the State Budget (to cover the taxation aspect) and the central planning mechanism (to cover the economic reforms). As the existing theories of public finance and taxation in the 'West' did not provide such a perspective, I took a lesson from the new 'institutional economics' (markets versus hierarchies) to develop a theory of State intervention which embraced the role of central planning, the State Budget, and the market mechanism. In this context, I have stood what, in some circles, passes for conventional wisdom of comparative economic systems on its head: I have argued that plan and market are complementary allocative mechanisms, rather than competing ones. I also argue the case for central planning on efficiency grounds, rather than proclaiming its general inefficiency, as some commentators have done. Within this same institutional perspective, I was able to develop a theory of economic reform as organisational change, and provide explanations of the economic forces leading to reforms, and of the economic causes of the frequent failure of reforms.

Against this background, I went on to distil the experience of taxation and budgetary policy of individual centrally planned economies into general stereotypes (or 'models') of taxation in 'command' economies and in economic reforms. I spend a little time contrasting this with the more complex budgetary systems of selected socialist countries, but very little of the book is devoted to empirical study - partly because the data is sometimes incomplete, but more particularly because I felt that country by country case-studies would not give me the general perspective which I sought.

Out of my general stereotype, I picked out three areas of taxation and budgetary policy. These were: sales taxation and price policy; wage taxation and wage policy; and taxes on capital and profits. I then provide a commentary on the economic effects of taxation policies, drawn partly from the institutional perspective, and partly from the economic theory of public finance. The analysis is generally based on a short-run, partial equilibrium nature, and provides some useful theoretical insights into the role of taxation in a socialist economy.

The overall slant of the book is theoretical, devoted to outlining the functions and effects of socialist taxation in general, and selected types of taxation in particular. This is done by setting these taxes against a more general theory of the management of the socialist economy. The result is a book which breaks new ground in the theory of the socialist economy. However, much work remains to be done. I have outlined my ideas on the directions future work might take in the last chapter.

Chapter 1

TAXATION AND CENTRAL PLANNING

WHY 'SOCIALIST' TAXATION?

Economists working in the field of comparative economic systems have generally neglected the question of taxation in socialist countries. The only general studies have been Holzman (1954) and Musgrave (1969) although a translation of a Yugoslav study has recently been published - Jurkovicz 1982/83, and Sobbrio (1982) provides a brief note on fiscal policy and socialist economic reforms. Other studies, such as Adam, 1974, have concentrated on selected aspects of taxation, especially turnover tax and pricing policy.

The neglect of socialist taxation is somewhat surprising. In economies like Britain and the USA, the study of taxation is important because of its impact on resource allocation and income distribution. Studies of socialist economies, however, have concentrated on the role of central planning in allocation and distribution, so neglecting an important mechanism whereby the State regulates economic activity.

The aim of this book is to restore the study of taxation to its rightful role in comparative economic studies. Taxation and the State Budget are here regarded as tools of economic policy which complement central economic planning. Firstly, taxation and the State Budget are major elements in the system of financial planning which complements economic planning. Secondly, taxation supplies funds to the budgetary sector, which is an important supplier of goods and services (in 'capitalist' and 'socialist' countries alike). Thirdly, taxation of socialised enterprises provides an important financial link between the central authorities and enterprises which can be used as a tool of economic policy.

Before proceeding to elaborate the economics of socialist taxation, we must first define the term more precisely. In a capitalist economy, taxation is a device for transferring control over resources from the private sector to the State (public) sector, in order that the State can carry out a limited range of economic functions (see Musgrave, 1959, esp. Ch.1; Brown and Jackson, 1982, Ch.2). In a socialist economy, the State has more extensive control over resources than the capitalist State. In this context, we use the term 'socialist economy' to mean one in which resources are owned collectively (usually by the State) and which is centrally planned in the sense that the State consciously tries to control, direct and influence the production and distribution of economic goods and services. In such an economy, the private sector's economic role is primarily one of supplying labour and consuming. Taxation is not generally required to effect a transfer of ownership of resources, since the State already has wide-ranging ownership and control.

Thus one might argue, as the Marxist theory of the State does (e.g. Sanderson, 1969, ch.4; Foley, 1978), that taxation will simply wither away in a socialist state. In this approach, taxation in capitalist countries is an instrument for the exploitation and subjugation of the proletariat. The State, acting in the interests of the capitalist class, levies taxes to finance expenditures which are designed to discipline and control the working class (e.g. police, army, judiciary), to reproduce a suitably equipped work force (e.g. health care, education and training) and to pacify the working-classes, such as State welfare benefits . From this, it is easy to argue that taxation will eventually vanish from a socialist economy, on the grounds that class antagonism will no longer exist, and the State will operate in the interests of the working-class, not against them. Taxation, if it exists at all, is either a relic of the past which will eventually be abolished, or is a means of penalising any residual private enterprise.

Yet the State Budgets of socialist countries

are funded, to a large extent, by payments in the form of turnover 'tax', profits 'tax', etc., paid by socialised enterprises. Since the levying of the taxes involves no change of ownership, taxes on socialised enterprises are often seen as more akin to dividends (Floyd, 1978) to transfer payments (Wilczynski, 1973, pp. 116) or to the drawings of an owner from his/her business (Fedorowicz, 1968). Bird (1964, pp.204-205) has stated that the distinction between taxes on the sales of socialised enterprises, and the profits of such enterprises is an arbitrary one, while Holzman (1954) argues that both the taxes on socialised enterprises, and their after-tax profits, must be reckoned as part of the burden of taxation on the citizens of socialist countries. In both cases, the argument is that taxes paid to the State Budget and after-tax profits of enterprises represent the State's claims over resources which pre-empt the consumption rights of citizens.

However, other authors argue that a tax on socialised enterprises is a particular method of transferring control over the disposal of funds from the enterprise to the State (budgetary) sector, and that the tax method has certain characteristics which distinguish it from other types of transfers (Weralski, 1973, pp.204-209; Kaleta, 1977, pp.99-101). These characteristics resemble those of taxes in capitalist economies, and may be summarised as follows:

1. The tax is a general obligation, applying to all economic units of a defined type.
2. The tax is not repayable (unless excess tax has been collected in error).
3. Payment of tax does not establish a claim for particular goods and services by the tax-payer.
4. Payment is compulsory.
5. Liability to tax is non-arbitrary and in accordance with pre-established rules laid down by the State.

The author believes that socialist taxation may be viewed as a method of transferring funds, and control over resources from socialist enterprises to the State Budget. In addition, a socialist state can, of course, also levy taxes on individual citizens and on any residual private sector, in the same way as a capitalist state does. Thus, socialism can be viewed as extending the role of budgetary policy in the economy.

ALLOCATIVE MECHANISMS: PLAN, MARKET AND BUDGET

In discussing questions of resource allocation from a comparative economic perspective, it is usual to classify economies as 'market economies' or 'planned economies'. A market economy is defined as one in which the dominant mechanism for resource allocation is the Market. A planned economy is one in which the dominant mechanism for resource allocation is the Plan. A third category is often added: the mixed economy, to cover those 'market' economies in which there is a substantial Budget sector, so that there is a mixture of 'market' and 'non-market' allocation.

The present author feels that this approach is somewhat deficient. Firstly, all economies, whether 'socialist' or 'capitalist', are 'mixed' to some extent. As Williamson (1975) and Galbraith (1969, 1975) among others, have pointed out, the firm in a capitalist economy constitutes a planning system, in that the Market is not used to allocate resources within the firm. (This approach follows pioneering work by Coase, 1937). Secondly, 'planned economies' have, in fact, two kinds of non-market allocation mechanism: the (National) Plan and the (State) Budget. To concentrate on the Plan and ignore the Budget, presents a seriously distorted picture. Montias (1976, p.115) is one author who has acknowledged the role which the Budget plays in centrally planned economies, but his main purpose in doing so was to refine his definition of an enterprise, and the role of the Budget as an allocative mechanism was otherwise given scant attention. Nevertheless, Montias provides a useful distinction between financially autonomous enterprises and non-autonomous budget organisations (or bureaus), which opens up the possibility of discussing different types of non-market allocation, and diferent types of activity by the State.

We shall continue to define a socialist

economy as one which the State both owns, and consciously tries to control, the productive resources in the economy. As a background to the role of taxation, we need to explain why the socialist State adopts two forms of non-market allocation, and why it might be deemed necessary to circumscribe the role of the market. This is a massive task in itself, and to simplify, we shall concentrate only on the economic reasons for State interference in, and/or control of, resource allocation. Thus we ignore arguments for socialism based on income distribution and social justice, and arguments based on the instability of the market economy. We ignore political and historical theories about socialism, in order to concentrate on what economic theory has to say about the role of the State. We then expand this to draw some conclusions about taxation.

For expositional purposes, let us assume that, in any economy, there exist three mechanisms for allocating resources. These may be summarised as: the Market; the Plan; and the Budget. Again for expositional purposes, let us assume that the economy can be divided into three distinct sectors, each of which uses only one of the three allocative mechanisms.

In the Market sector, resources are allocated by means of autonomous contracts agreed between buyers and sellers of goods and services. The 'autonomy' of the contracts has a variety of implications. Firstly, the contractors are autonomous individuals in that they may freely enter into any contract they consider to be in their own best interests. Secondly, the contracts are autonomous, in that terms of each contract are independent of any other contract made. Thirdly, economic action is undertaken as the result of the agreement of a contract. Fourthly, any action resulting from a contract is solely determined by the terms of the contract. Fifthly, revenues and costs arising from economic action resulting from a contract determine the income (profit or loss) received by the actor.

In the Plan sector, resources are allocated by groups of actors, organised as 'firms'. Members of a firm cooperate to implement an overall Plan for allocation. The Plan is a set of pre-determined actions aimed at achieving pre-selected goals. Goals and actions are set by a group of Planners. Planners may be members of the firm, or they may constitute a separate organisation. The Plans which they devise may cover the activities of a single firm, or may coordinate the activities of a number of firms. The Planners and the firm(s) to which the Plan applies constitute a planning system. Within the planning system, actors act in response to instructions issued by the Planners; they do not initiate action on their own account. Actions of individuals are inter-dependent, linked through the Plan, and result in the incurring of costs (in production) and the earning of revenues (through sale of output). Firms are financially autonomous units, in that costs and revenues determine the income (profit or loss) of the firm as a whole. Income of individual members, on the other hand, does not depend on the costs and revenues for which they are personally responsible, but is determined in some other way (e.g. a defined 'rate for the job').

In the Budget sector, resources are allocated by groups of actors organised into 'bureaus'. 'Bureaus' are not financially autonomous. The bureau's costs are covered by a grant from a larger parent organisation which sets the goals of the bureau. Members of the bureau spend the grant in order to achieve those goals. The bureau's income is determined by its grant, not by the revenues and costs associated with its activities. The output of the bureau is not normally sold but given away to clients. (Any revenue which a bureau does earn accrues to the parent organisation, forming part of its income).

Nevertheless, there are also some similarities between bureaus and firms. Within these organisations, resources are allocated by a non-market mechanism. Actors do not enter into contracts on their own account, but act in response to instructions from superiors (planners in the case of firms, the parent organisation in the case of bureaus). These instructions form part of some overall design. Each individual's actions are part of some larger whole. Income of individual actors is not determined by the revenues she/he earns, nor the costs she/he incurs. In the Plan and Budget sector, economic action is based on cooperation between individuals, and on collective goals. In the Market sector, action is based on rivalry and competition between individuals, and on the pursuit of individual self-interest.

The justification for non-market allocation has been discussed by a variety of economists. Public finance theory has analysed reasons for budgetary allocation, while the case for planning has recently been argued by the new 'institutional economics'. Comparative economics, on the other hand, has tended to neglect the budgetary sector, while concentrating on the case for central planning. The present author has found it more fruitful to draw on branches of economics other than comparative economics.

In the economic theory of public finance, the case for budgetary provision of goods and services is usually based on the concept of 'market failure', to which a wide literature has been devoted (for example, Musgrave, 1959, pp.6-17; Musgrave, 1971; Steiner, 1974, pp.243-257; Brown and Jackson, 1982, pp.24-33; 40-67). Basically, the argument is that the special characteristics of some goods prevent their optimal supply through the market mechanism. For some goods, consumer preference revelation is imperfect and demand schedules do not reflect marginal social benefit (e.g. public goods, goods generating positive externalities, and merit goods). Private producers thus lack appropriate signals to lead them to produce optimally. Where markets are imperfect, prices are imperfect, and allocation is sub-optimal. For other goods, the price charged by a profit-maximising firm would not be equal to marginal social cost (e.g. declining-cost industries, goods generating negative externalities, goods with zero marginal cost, such as a bridge). For all these goods, market allocation would violate conditions for welfare optima. Theory argues for public subsidy, financing or regulation of such goods, and the argument is often taken to imply state supply of such goods through its own budgetary activities.

The case for planning which is found in the new institutional economics is perhaps less well-known. Those theories are concerned with internal allocation of resources, where allocation is planned by the Planners at Head

Office, rather than mediated through exchange of autonomous contracts in the market. The firm itself is treated as a planning system. The best known and most developed theory is probably found in the work of O.E. Williamson. Williamson (1975, especially Ch.2) has argued that firms adopt internal resource allocation because, in some circumstances, it is a least-cost, efficient allocation, compared to market allocation. Market allocation is relatively inefficient, Williamson claims, when certain environmental and human factors interact, particularly the combinations of uncertainty with bounded rationality, and of opportunism with small numbers exchange.

The combination of uncertainty with bounded rationality makes long-term market contracting a more expensive allocative mechanism than internal decision-making. Uncertainty simply reflects inability to know future events, and, of itself, does not prevent long-term contracting, provided complete insurance markets exist. With perfect insurance markets, contracts can be written to cover every contingency, and expected costs and revenues can be calculated. However, perfect insurance markets do not exist; insurance markets fail because of bounded rationality (a concept taken from H.A. Simon, 1961, who used it in the context of the 'satisficing' theory of firm behaviour). Bounded rationality arises because individuals possess imperfect foresight, and limited capacity to recognise, absorb and process information. As a result, possible outcomes of economic activities cannot be specified in full, and insurance markets are incomplete. It is unrealistic to expect individuals to 'optimise', in the neo-classical sense. Bounded rationality leads to 'adaptive' rather than 'optimising' behaviour. A solution is worked out in the light of available information, but revised as new information becomes available. This contrasts with the contracting solution, in which resources are committed once and for all by the terms of contract.

Internal decision-making, rather than long-term market contracting, permits cost-savings.

Firstly, some bargaining costs are avoided.

Secondly, the firm saves on administrative costs, particularly search costs and information costs, by making sequential adaptive decisions, with limited information, rather than trying to establish an optimum solution.

Thirdly, the firm avoids losses arising from misallocation of resources associated with being 'locked into' long-term contracts based on imperfect information and imperfect market signals. Revision of allocation decisions is simpler by internal allocation, compared with trying to renegotiate a contract.

Fourthly, communication costs are lower within organisations, since in-house codes and jargon emerge, and there is less opportunity for ambiguity and misunderstanding which could lead to misallocation.

Fifthly, internal allocation promotes convergence of expectations, through a central coordinating mechanism, so avoiding losses due to misallocation arising from inconsistent expectations and incompatible decisions of parties to market contracts.

Turning from long-term to short-term contracting, the problem is the combination of opportunism and small numbers exchange. Opportunism is lack of candour or honesty in bargaining. Parties to a contract may supply selective or distorted information to gain advantage. If large numbers of competitive rivals were involved, opportunism would not impede the operation of the market. But where small numbers bargaining (oligopoly) prevails, market rivalry is a less effective check, and there is more scope for opportunistic haggling. This haggling may promote the interests of individual contractors, but, as Williamson observes, (1975, p.27) 'the interests of the <u>system</u>, by contrast, are promoted if the parties can be joined in such a way as to avoid both the bargaining costs and the indirect costs (mainly maladaptation costs) which are generated in the process'. (Opportunistic behaviour is, of course, not unknown even within planning systems).

Internal decision-making as a replacement for short-term contracting reduces costs in a variety of ways.

Firstly, the parties concerned are not rivals for profit, but joint profit-maximisers. Hence the gains from prolonging any haggling are lower than would be the case for market exchange, and internal bargaining costs are lower.

Secondly, it is easier to check the reliability of information, and uncover opportunism, by means of a firm's internal audit, than it is to audit another firm externally. Individuals are more likely to be cooperative in the case of internal audit (and to be rewarded for it).

Thirdly, internal disputes are more easily settled than disputes between rival market traders. The parties are more likely to be cooperative, expensive litigation is less likely, and, if necessary, a higher authority within the organisation can simply step in and impose a solution.

The Williamson model is not in itself a model, or a recommendation, of central planning. Nevertheless, it has some interesting implications for central planning. Williamson uses his model to point out potential efficiency gains from vertical, horizontal and conglomerate mergers of firms. These same efficiency gains, it may be argued, can be reaped by a central planning system in which the whole economy is organised as a single organisation.

This approach would argue for central planning and, by implication, for 'socialism' on the grounds of economic efficiency. In this context, it is interesting to note that Williamson seems to be arguing that central planners are likely to have better information, and allocate resources more efficiently, than market operators. This contrasts with the criticism made of centrally planned economies, that they are likely to be inefficient, compared to market economies. This view was put forward by, among others, von Hayek and von Mises (Hayek, 1935). They argued that, in the absence of a competitive market system, central planners would lack complete information on prices, and planning was necessarily inefficient, since it would be impractical to calculate all the necessary accounting prices.

Yet it has long been argued that, without a central co-ordinating mechanism, such as a Walrasian auctioneer, even competitive markets may fail to converge on equilibrium. Without an auctioneer, 'false trading' (exchange at non-equilibrium prices) can occur, and if resources are allocated on the basis of non-equilibrium prices, resource allocation is necessarily inefficient. (For discussion of 'false trading' and disequilibrium economics, see Barro and

Grossman, 1976).

Williamson's approach recognises that both bounded rationality, and opportunism are likely to lead to false trading. The world is unlikely to generate condition for perfect markets (or perfect planning, for that matter). The ideal allocative mechanism is one which produces a least-cost, least-inefficient solution. However, Williamson's approach does not imply that planning is always superior to market allocation. Transactions will be the subject of market allocation if the conditions causing market failure are absent e.g. where large numbers exchange prevails. Thus we should expect all economies to be 'mixed economies'.

Drawing together the arguments of this section, it is argued that, in the Budget sector, non-market allocation is adopted because of the special characteristics of certain goods, which make them unmarketable by normal market processes. In the Plan sector, on the other hand, goods are marketable, but internal allocation is preferred to market allocation on efficiency grounds, and planning system is preferable to a set of independent market transactions. In the Budget sector, the non-marketability of output means that supply is funded by grants, and supplying organisations are organised as bureaus, lacking financial autonomy. In the Plan sector, output is marketable, supplying organisations can cover costs of production from sales revenue, and can be organised as financially autonomous firms. Here we have the basis for an explanation of two different kinds of non-market allocation.

FURTHER FUNCTIONS OF THE BUDGET SECTOR

In the Budget sector, the problem of financing bureaus arises. In the Critique of the Gotha Programme, Marx (1974, pp.23-24) treated the financing of 'that which is intended for the satisfaction of common needs' (e.g. schools, hospitals, etc.), as part of a more general problem of the division of social product in a future socialist state. This, perhaps, points the way to a difference in the role of the Budget sector in a socialist society, compared to capitalist one.

In a capitalist society, the income of

the Budget sector, in the form of taxation, represents confiscation of resources from the Market and Plan sectors. In a socialist society, such confiscation is no longer required. Instead, the Budget is used as an instrument for the division of national income among various uses (Blass and Fedorowicz, 1968). These uses may be classified broadly as individual consumption, collective consumption, and investment. Income gathered to the Budget is disbursed to apportion control over resources throughout the whole economy. Budget and Plan are closely linked. (For the time being, the Market is ignored). The Plan directs the output of marketed goods, the Budget controls the distribution of the cash flow generated by marketed output, and plans the output of non-marketed goods, earmarked for collective consumption.

Furthermore, the Budget complements wage policy in regulating the inter-personal distribution of income. The budgetary instruments at the State's disposal include social security policy, indirect taxation on consumer goods, which influences the level and structure of retail prices, and direct taxation of personal incomes. The Budget thus has a distributional function, as well as an allocative one.

Economic stabilisation is also a function of the Budget under socialism. The Budget is a major influence on financial and monetary flows because of its role in the division of national incomes, and is therefore a major tool for securing monetary and financial equilibrium. The Budget forms part of the system of financial planning, which aims to balance flows of funds and purchasing power against available flows of goods.

Because of the importance of monetary and financial flows to and from the Budget, these flows are important information sources for Central Planners, and the Budget constitutes part of the control mechanism of the economy. Budgetary flows may be used to monitor the performance of the economy providing feedback on the achievement of Plans, and indicating possible needs for remedial action if Plans are failing.

Finally, the terms on which funds are transferred between socialised enterprises and the Budget, provide a way of sending instructions to producers which is an alternative to issuing administrative directives. Tax and subsidy policy generate financial signals, which can be used for 'indirect' management of enterprises by Central Planners. This use of financial instruments is a feature of economic reform models, discussed in later chapters.

SUMMARY

This chapter began by discussing the appropriate definition of taxation in a socialist economy where the State already has extensive powers to control resource allocation through social ownership of the means of production and the mechanism of central planning. Taxation was viewed as a particular method of transferring financial resources, and control over real resources, from State enterprise to central Planners. It was argued that central planning was one of three complementary allocative mechanisms open to a socialist government, namely, Plan, Market and Budget. Particular emphasis was laid on the essentially complementary nature of the three mechanisms, and on the efficiency gains which could be reaped by using central planning. The State Budget, and its income in the form of taxation, was viewed not only as an allocative mechanism, but also as a tool for redistributing control over resources in the process of the division of national income, as a tool of stabilisation policy through financial planning, as a tool of income distribution, and as part of the system of financial control.

REFERENCES

ADAM, J. (1974) Price and Taxation Policy in Czechoslovakia 1948-70 Duncker and Humblot, Berlin

BARRO, R.J. and GROSSMAN, H.I. (1976), Money, Employment and Inflation Cambridge University Press

BIRD, R. (1964) 'The Possibility of Fiscal Harmonisation in the Communist Bloc' Public Finance Vol.19, No.3, pp.201-224

BLASS, B. and FEDOROWICZ, Z. (1968) 'The Role of the State Budget in the Intersectoral and Interdivisional Distribution of Income in the People's Republic of Poland' Public Finance Vol.23, No.1-2, pp.106-123

BROWN, C.V. and JACKSON, P.M. (1982), 2nd ed Public Sector Economics Martin Robertson, Oxford, 1982

COASE, R.H. (1937) 'The Nature of the Firm' Economica Vol.4, pp.386-405; reprinted in G.J. Stigler and K.E. Boulding (eds.) (1952) Readings in Price Theory Richard D. Irwin, inc., Homewood, Illinois

FEDOROWICZ, Z. (1968) 'The Role of Finance In a Socialist Economy' in Z. Fedorowicz et al. Finances and Banking: a collection of papers and articles State Economic Publishers, Warsaw

FLOYD, R. (1978) 'Some Aspects of Income Taxation of Public Enterprises' International Monetary Fund Staff Papers Vol.25, No.2, pp.310-343

FOLEY, D.K. (1978) 'State Expenditure from a Marxist Perspective' Journal of Public Economics Vol.9, No.2, pp.221-238

HAYEK, F.A. (ed.)(1935) Collective Economic Planning Macmillan, London

HOLZMAN, F.D. (1954) Soviet Taxation Harvard University Press, Cambridge, Mass

JURKOVICZ, P. (1982/83) 'Content and Characteristics of the Public Financing System' Eastern European Economics Vol.21, No.2, pp.3-49

KALETA, J. (1977) Budgetary Economics (Polish) State Economic Publishers, Warsaw

MARX, K. (1974) Critique of the Gotha Programme Foreign Language Press, Peking

MONTIAS, J.M. (1976) The Structure of Economic Systems Yale University Press, Newhaven and London

MUSGRAVE, R.A. (1959) The Theory of Public Finance Mc-Graw-Hill Kogakusha International Student Edition, Tokyo, 1959

MUSGRAVE, R.A. (1969) Fiscal Systems Yale University Press, New Haven, Conn.

MUSGRAVE, R.A. (1971) 'Provision for Social Goods in a Market System' Public Finance Vol.26, No.2, pp.304-320

SANDERSON, J.B. (1969) An Interpretation of the Political Ideas of Marx and Engels Longmans Green, London

SIMON, H.A. (1961) Administrative Behaviour 2nd ed., Macmillan, New York

SOBBRIO, G. (1982) 'Some Notes on Economic

Reforms and Fiscal Policy in Socialist Countries' Economic Notes No.1, pp.85-93
STEINER, P.O. (1974) 'Public Expenditure Budgeting' in A. Blinder et al. The Economics of Public Finance Brookings Institution, Washington D.C., 1974
WERALSKI, M. (1973) 'Problems of Budgetary Policy in Socialist Planned Economies' in W.L. David (ed.) Public Finance, Planning and Economic Development: Essays in Honour of Ursula Hicks Macmillan, London
WILCZYNSKI, J. (1973) Profit, Risk and Incentives under Socialist Planning Macmillan, London and New York
WILLIAMSON, O.E. (1975) Markets and Hierarchies: Analysis and Anti-Trust Implications Free Press, New York

Chapter 2

MANAGEMENT OF THE SOCIALIST ECONOMY

STEERING MECHANISM

The term steering mechanism (or economic mechanism) refers to the arrangements whereby the State apparatus seeks to control the allocation of resources. As Kornai (1971, p.54) has pointed out, the term is not a very precise one, but it basically encompasses two characteristics. Firstly, it includes a set of economic organisations. Secondly, it covers what Kornai calls "the response function system of the control sphere, which includes economic management at every level" (p.54). The response function is "the relationship between the input entering the unit and the unit's initial state, on the one hand, and the output leaving the unit, and the change in the unit's state" (p.45). Kornai takes a broad view of inputs (pp.47-50) which include not only real goods but also information - which could be prices, plan directives, customers' orders - whatever induces the unit (economic organisation) to produce outputs. Interestingly, Kornai does not mention finance as an input, although it is a necessary one in a monetary economy.

In a centrally planned economy, the State consciously builds the steering mechanism, creating economic organisations and issuing them with a response function chosen by the State. The creation of a steering mechanism is an attempt to create a framework for policy implementation, whereby the State 'drives' the economy along its planned route. As Dunsire (1978) has pointed out, in a bureaucracy of any type, policy implementation requires operationalisation of a decision by translating the general policy into specific operating instructions. Dunsire's example is the policy decision to close a Yorkshire railway line, which was made operational by instructions about date and time of the last train, notices to be issued to the public, retimetabling, salvaging of railway property, blocking tunnels, removal of track etc. The socialist state makes its policy operational through its chosen steering mechanism.

The organisations of the steering mechanisms are the organisations of what, in Chapter 1, we called the Plan sector. In the industrial sector of centrally planned economies of the Soviet Union and Eastern Europe, the term 'socialised industry' is used. Generally speaking, socialised industry is organised in a four-tier hierarchy. At the bottom, there are socialised enterprises (or firms), which are the basic financially autonomous units producing goods and services. Autonomy of enterprises is restricted since they are grouped together in industry-wide State corporations (also known as trusts, associations, or large economic organisations). Corporations also have financial autonomy, and enterprises have a status akin to that of departments or divisions of a large British or American company. The position and role of the corporation is not always very clear. Their powers over constituent enterprises vary (Woodall, 1982, Chs.3,4). Gomulka (1983, p.4) reports that Poland has abolished its corporations, though "177 new organisations were formed, of which 45 are obligatory ... Their main function is to serve member firms as agents organising supplies, sales and R & D activities .. they have no direct management powers, but may exercise an indirect influence" (pp.3-4). Hare (1983, p.324) reports on a small number of attempts to break up large Hungarian corporations into smaller units.

Corporations are subordinate to a Branch Ministry, responsible for a particular economic sector. Branch Ministries represent an intermediate layer of State administration. Their main function is to transmit information between corporations and central planners. In the 'command' model of the socialist economy (see pp.20-23 below), they play a particular role in 'plan disaggregation', by translating centrally defined industry targets into specific corporate targets. Branch Ministries are thus subordinate to the authority of central planners, who constitute the top layer of the hierarchy.

One of the most striking features of the economic organisation of CPEs has been increasing industrial concentration, as a result of horizontal and vertical integration. Woodall (1982, p.111) has attributed these mergers to 'taut planning and a seller's market which incur uncertain supplies and poor markets for intermediate products', as well as to a desire to reap economies of scale in administration, planning, research and development, investment and sales. Some echoes of Williamson are awakened; he has specifically stressed the administrative advantages of hierarchical organisations, and the advantages of internal organisation over intermediate product markets, as a motivating force for integration, particularly vertical integration „(1975, Chs. 5 and 6, and Ch.7, p.117). Hohman (1982, p.3) stresses that increasing concentration facilitates central planning, by reducing the number of organisations to be co-ordinated. However, the effects of concentration may not be entirely beneficial, and the Eastern European model has given rise to some diseconomies of scale, including dysfunctional managerial behaviour, such as the labour hoarding discussed on p.24 and p.96.

The response function system varies according to the type of steering mechanism. We shall treat production as a response to information received by managers of State corporations. In the traditional 'command economy' mechanism (see next section of this chapter) this information consists of instructions from central planners. However, pressure for economic reform represents pressure for a different type of response function, in which information is received in the form of economic signals, such as prices, taxes, customers' orders, etc. and managers are basically given the task of maximising profit. This requires organisational changes, involving greater delegation of management powers to lower levels.

Williamson has dealt with the question of organisational change in the context of "markets versus hierarchies". In this approach, firms adopt a hierarchical form of organisation because it economises on transaction costs, compared to both autonomous market transactions, and to simple co-operative work groups (1975, Ch.3). However, the organisational form of the hierarchy also reflects transaction costs (Chs.7,8). Initially, the firm adopts a unitary form (U-form) of organisation, along functional lines. Head office is responsible for day-to-day operating management, for strategic long-term planning, and for control of the activities of a number of functional departments (such as manufacturing, sales, finance etc.). As the firm grows larger, however, transactional diseconomies occur, principally caused by the bounded rationality of head office management. The resulting finite span of control means that, as the firm grows, with organisational form held constant, management control eventually breaks down. As the firm grows larger, and more levels are added to the hierarchy, there is distortion and loss of information as it moves through the hierarchy, due to the editing and summarising of data, and the operationalisation of instructions. Head office becomes more remote from lower-level personnel, who consequently feel less moral involvement in the firm, and identify less with its goals. Such phenomena intensify the loss of control.

According to Williamson, these transactional diseconomies can be reduced by reorganising the firm in a multi-divisional (or M-form) structure. In the M-form firm, head office delegates operating powers to the managers of a number of autonomous divisions or profit centres, retaining strategic tasks such as long-term planning and control over internal transfer pricing. There are similarities between a capitalist corporation shifting from U-form to M-form, and a centrally planned economy adopting a more decentralised form of steering mechanism as a result of economic reforms, as we shall see later in the chapter.

Whatever the steering mechanism adopted, the role of taxation lies in the response function system. Firstly, tax rates and tax regulations are pieces of information which enter an economic organisation as an input. Secondly, taxes paid leave the organisation as an output. Thirdly, taxes determine the organisation's net residual profit, which, in some mechanisms, is an element in the finance at the disposal of the organisation's management. In addition tax revenue finances the budgetary sector, where organisations take the form of grant-funded bureaus.

THE COMMAND MECHANISM

Probably the most common stereotype of the centrally planned economy is the 'command economy' which operates with a steering mechanism based on a highly centralised form of planning. In the extreme stereotype, all economic activity is controlled by instructions from the Central Planners, who plan the level and structure of output in detail, work out the tasks which must be performed to fulfil the plan, and issue instructions in the form of plan directives, targets, obligatory indices, etc. A system of economic administration transmits these instructions, from Planners to Branch Ministries, from Ministries to managers of State corporations and enterprises, and eventually down to individual factories and the shop floor. At each stage, instructions are operationalised by a process of plan disaggregation. At Ministry level, instructions addressed to a whole sector are broken down into instructions addressed to corporations; the corporate head office breaks instructions down into a form suitable for addressing to enterprises, and so on. In theory, lower levels have no discretion over production decision, and all decisions must be referred to the centre for approval. Prices, wages, exchange rates and interest rates, even the accounting rules on the depreciation of fixed assets, are all administered centrally.

In this stereotype, the whole economy is organised as one gigantic unitary or U-form corporation (to use Williamson's term). The Central Planners act as a head office, controlling both day-to-day operating decisions and long-term strategic decisions. In practice, of course, no large organisation, be it an M-form corporation, or a socialist economy, can really take all decisions at Head Office/ Central Planning level. However, we assume that lower-level decision-making is regarded by 'Head Office' as relating to minor matters and limited in scope. As a result, lower-level management is regarded as 'administration' (the carrying out of orders from supervisors) rather than as management per se, which may be regarded as initiating allocative processes.

In the command economy, planning is geared to the structure and size of output. Plan targets are output-based, 'specialised' indicators of performance, usually the quantity or value of output. The criterion of economic success is whether these plan targets are achieved. To motivate workers and managers, bonuses are paid for achieving plan targets, and even larger bonuses for exceeding them. Moral incentives are also used e.g. the award of titles, medals and decorations; 'league tables' of levels of output; publicity given to model workers. These moral incentives are also geared to rewarding fulfilment and overfulfilment of the Plan.

In the command economy, taxation is relatively unimportant. Taxation of enterprises supplies funds to the State Budget, but does not affect the behaviour of producers, except in so far as sales taxes influence the price and value of output; where plan targets are specified in quantity terms, sales taxes have no effect. (However, sales taxes determine retail prices, and influence the behaviour of consumers).

Occasionally, in an attempt to motivate efficiency, plan targets are expressed in terms of profit, and, if taxes influence measured profit, they can influence producer behaviour. Enterprises' residual profits are normally transferred to the State Budget in the command system, so taxes do not influence the financial resources of enterprises or corporations.

The command mechanism is criticised as defective, in a number of ways. Firstly, it may be argued that the command mechanism is inefficient, because it encourages producers to behave as bonus maximisers so that output is produced without taking account of the quality of goods, or the cost of producing them.

Secondly, it may be alleged that the command mechanism neglects the interests of consumers, since output is shaped by planners' preferences, rather than producers. The impact of planners' preferences is discussed by Ward (1961), Thornton (1976) and Montias

(1976), but the concept is a controversial one, and some authors (e.g. Nove, 1979) questioned the idea that planners' preferences will give rise to a pattern of output which differs from that consistent with consumer preferences. Yet, if we move outside comparative economics, the view that planners neglect the consumer interest is quite common; it is found, for example, in Galbraith's work on the modern corporation as a planning system (1969 and 1975), and in Niskanen's work on public sector bureaucracy (1968 and 1973).

Thirdly, it is alleged that the massive amount of detail involved in central planning makes the system unworkable and inefficient. This view was expressed in the 1930s by Hayek and von Mises, among others (Hayek, 1935), and has been vigorously expressed by Nove in more recent years (e.g. 1983).

These problems are essentially caused by the uncertainty of the economic environment, and the bounded rationality of central planners, on the other, and create pressures for institutional change which may be regarded as underlying pressures for economic reforms.

Fourthly, there are problems of distortion of information as it moves through the steering mechanism (Ellman, 1978). Central planners require data on which to base plans. This data is collected from producers, and transmitted upwards through the administrative hierarchy. At each stage, there is information loss as data are summarised and edited, and there is information distortion, as subordinates try to present themselves in the best possible light to superiors, even to the extent of reporting on the operation of factories which have not yet been opened, according to a much publicised report in Pravda some years ago. Each unit in the lower levels has a monopoly of certain types of information, and, in supplying information, is often trying to bargain over plan targets e.g. by exaggerating shortages of productive capacity of labour in order to obtain 'easy' targets. Command systems thus encounter problems of small number bargaining and opportunism. Even within the 'U-form', these factors combine to create what Williamson calls 'information impactedness' which 'exists when the true underlying circumstances relevant to the transaction ... are known to one or more parties, but cannot be costlessly discerned by or displayed for others' (1975, p.31). Information impactedness, combined with opportunistic behaviour by lower level personnel, places limits on vertical integration and the expansion of the U-form corporation, since information distortion reduces the efficiency of resource allocation.

The command mechanism used by centrally planned economies in the 1950s, was highly successful in mobilising resources for industrialisation, and high rates of economic growth were achieved. One explanation is the relative efficiency of internal decision-making, and the U-form of organisation. However, more recently, declining rates of economic growth have been a problem for the socialist economies of the Soviet Union and Eastern Europe (Drewnowski, 1982). From Williamson's theory of organisational change and the growth of the corporation, this was predictable. Transactional diseconomies (see p.19 above) increase as the size of the organisation grows, with organisational form held constant. Problems of bounded rationality, uncertainty, opportunism and information impactedness eventually limit the growth of the U-form socialist economy, creating pressure for organisational change. We shall interpret economic reforms in that light.

ECONOMIC REFORM OF THE STEERING MECHANISM

Economic reform is a general term describing changes in the steering mechanism of the socialist economy. We shall make the term economic reform more precise by using it to refer to the kind of changes attempted in various centrally planned economies from the late 1950s onwards, consisting principally of a reduction in detailed, centralised decision-making, and greater financial independence and operating discretion for managers of State corporations. The author's experience of these reforms is principally derived from a detailed study of the Polish reforms of 1973-75 (Wanless, 1980) and from a smaller study of Hungarian reforms in 1968 (Hare and Wanless, 1981). The essential features of these reformed steering mechanisms were:

(1) The number and scope of obligatory plan targets were reduced.
(2) Managers were instructed to maximise profits (or some related 'synthetic' indicator of performance).
(3) Managers were delegated powers to take operating decisions, e.g. level of current output, product mix, etc. Central planners retained control over strategic decisions e.g. broad divisions of national income between individual and collective consumption, and investment.
(4) A system of incentives was established which linked employee remuneration to improved profit performance. The corporation, rather than the budget, became the beneficiary of residual net profit.
(5) Central planners sought to control operating decisions by influencing the arguments of the profit function.
(6) Price reforms were planned, to produce a more rational structure of prices as a basis for decision-making.

Generally, the reforms aimed to increase efficiency and to raise economic welfare by increasing consumer satisfaction. Judging performance on the basis of profits achieved was a central prop of the reforms. The new performance indicators encouraged producers to cut costs, discouraged the hoarding of labour and other inputs, and provided incentives to produce the goods that customers wanted, rather than producing goods to fulfil the Plan.

There were various 'reforms' attempted in the centrally planned economies of the Soviet Union and Eastern Europe in the 1960s and 1970s. (These are now quite widely documented, for example, in Nove et al., 1982, NATO, 1981). Within these reforms, two types of mechanism may be distinguished: selectively decentralised socialism, and market socialism. There are a number of differences between them.

Firstly, and most importantly, the market socialist mechanism allows producers a substantial degree of freedom in price formation, so that many prices are determined at corporate level, in the light of the markets in which the producers operate. In selectively decentralised socialism, the central authorities continue to regulate prices, either through centralised administration by the State Price Commission, or by administered rules of cost-plus pricing made binding on State Corporations.

Secondly, the market socialism mechanism goes further in giving greater power to managers of corporations, and in reducing the number and scope of plan targets. In the selectively decentralised mechanisms, managers have less power to undertake contracts with outsiders, and are subject to more plan targets than would be the case in market socialism.

Thirdly, market socialism relies more heavily on market relations and market forces to influence production directly, rather than through the intermediation of central planners.

Fourthly, market socialism represents an attempt to displace central planning as the steering mechanism of the economy, while selective decentralisation is intended to supplement central planning, not to replace it. The hope was that selective decentralisation would improve the quality of central planning, especially strategic planning, by freeing central planners from excessively detailed planning.

Reforms are often interpreted as involving a strengthening of the role of the Market, and a reduction in the role of the Plan, as allocative mechanisms. The present author believes that this interpretation should be treatd with caution. While managers have more scope for responding to signals from the market, as a result of their new response function, economic reform does not involve any obvious reduction in internal decision-making by producers, and consequently there may not be strengthening of the role of market transactions over the economy as a whole. Indeed, attempts at reform were often accompanied by increased industrial concentration. The formation of corporations by vertical and horizontal mergers among enterprises was a deliberate part of the reform policy. It thus appears to make greater sense to view reforms as a reorganisation of the planning system, rather than a dismantling of it.

Reforms were also further limited in their effectiveness because typically investment continued to be centrally planned, so that only transactions on 'current account' were affected by the reforms.

The economic reform movement has had only a limited success. Höhmann (1982, p.2) points out that most reforms have been of the selectively decentralised type. Market socialist reforms have been attempted only in Yugoslavia, Hungary and Czechoslovakia. The Czech reforms were abandoned after the crushing of the 'Prague spring' by the invasion of Warsaw Pact troops in 1968. Reforms of the selectively decentralised type have been attempted at various times in the 1960s and 1970s, by the USSR, GDR, Poland, Bulgaria, Romania, Czechoslovakia after 1968, and, tentatively, in Albania. However, the selectively decentralised reforms have tended to be short-lived, and rapidly abandoned in favour of recentralisation and a return to the command mechanism.

Many writers have discussed why selective decentralisation has failed (see the works on economic reform already cited). The present author, in a previous work (Wanless, 1980), attributed the failure of Polish attempts at selective decentralisation to bad timing, to administrative weaknesses and incompatibility of policy objectives. More generally, reform attempts have been characterised by a failure to implement price reforms, partial and selective implementation of the reformed mechanism, and the reluctance of the central authorities to abandon their role in operating management, so that managerial independence at corporate and enterprise level has continually been undermined by interference from the centre.

The causes of reform failure may be generalised, using concepts drawn from the theory of organisations, and applying them to the organisational relationships between economic institutions. Reform of the steering mechanism involves both changes in organisational relationships, and changes in the response function.

Organisationally, reform shifts the socialist economy away from the U-form into the M-form of organisation, with separation of strategic management (at head office or central planning level) and operating management (at corporate/enterprise level). Accompanying this organisational change, a new response function is introduced. Managers now respond to the arguments of the profit function (i.e. prices and quantities of goods), rather than to output targets. The central authorities try to steer the economy by influencing the arguments of the profit function, by means of various financial policy instruments, such as taxes.

Williamson (1975, pp.152-155) has stressed the advantages of M-form over U-form organisation in overcoming diseconomies of scale, but also stresses the conditions necessary to achieve M-form advantages. These are, firstly, separation of operating management from strategic management, and, secondly, establishing and systematically employing a suitable internal control apparatus. This may be contrasted with what Williamson calls a 'corrupted multi-divisional firm', which is 'a multi-divisional structure for which the requisite control apparatus has been provided, but in which the general management has become extensively involved in operating affairs. The appropriate distance relation thus is missing, with the result that M-form performance, over the long run, cannot reliably be expected' (p.153).

One plausible explanation of the failure of selective decentralisation is that it is not a genuine M-form of organisation, but only a corrupted M-form. Market socialism, on the other hand, is more like a genuine M-form, which can explain its greater success. It is notable that selectively decentralised reforms, on the whole, did not involve either formal or practical reduction in the powers of central planners over State corporations, exercised through Branch Ministries.

Furthermore, it was often unclear whether operating management was the responsibility of the corporation or the enterprise. For example, in the Polish 1973 reform, reform decrees issued by the Council of Ministers were addressed to corporations, but under the Polish constitution, the basic autonomous financial unit is the enterprise. The market socialist reforms seem to have succeeded in giving rather more independence to corporations. (For a contrast between Polish and Hungarian experience, see Hare and Wanless, 1981, pp.510-512. Note that Hungarian reforms have not gone as far as the present author's description of a market socialist mechanism).

Selective decentralisation thus appears

to fail on grounds of inappropriate organisational form, since it fails to take the socialist economy to full M-form status. Nove, 1983, has acknowledged the relevance of Williamson's work to the organisation of a socialist economy, particularly on the question of 'the range of decisions which "belong" at the level of the production unit, as distinct from the corporation headquarters' (p.202). Woodall comments on the weaknesses of Polish management structure, especially in the 1970s (1982, pp.97-107). Awareness of the organisational implications of reform provides important background to evaluating and understanding the policies, targets and instruments of reform.

SUMMARY

This chapter discusses the general problems of management of a socialist economy, in order to set the State Budget in context, and to show the framework of policy within which socialist taxation operated. Taxation, it was argued, formed part of the steering mechanism linking State and industry, and provided a mechanism whereby the State could influence industry without administrative direction. This kind of 'indirect' steering would, it was argued, be more important when economic reforms were undertaken than it would be in the traditional 'command' mechanism. Pressure for economic reforms, it was argued, arose because of mounting transactional diseconomies in the command system, which arose from its organisational form. Changes in organisational form, if successful, could result in an increase in economic efficiency; it was argued that the frequent failure of economic reforms had occurred because the selected organisational changes were inappropriate, and did not involve enough decentralisation.

REFERENCES

DUNSIRE, A. (1978) Implementation in a Bureaucracy (Vol.1 of The Executive Process), Martin Robertson, Oxford

DREWNOWSKI, J. (ed) Crisis in the World Economy: The Spread of the Polish Disease Croom

Helm, London
ELLMAN, M. (1978) 'The Fundamental Problem of Socialist Planning', Oxford Economic Papers Vol.30, No.2, pp.249-262
GALBRAITH, J.K. (1969) The New Industrial State Penguin, Harmondsworth
GALBRAITH, J.K. (1975) Economic and the Public Purpose Penguin, Harmondsworth
GOMULKA, S. (1983) 'Polish Economic Reforms: Principles, Practice, Prospects' Paper presented at the Annual Conference of the National Association for Soviet and East European Studies, Fitzwilliam College, Cambridge, March 26-28
HARE, P.G. (1983) 'The Beginnings of Institutional Reform in Hungary' Soviet Studies Vol.35, No.3, pp.313-330
HARE, P.G. and WANLESS, P.T. (1981) 'Polish and Hungarian Economic Reforms: A Comparison' Soviet Studies Vol.33, No.4, pp.491-517
HAYEK, F.A. (ed), Collectivist Economic Planning Macmillan, London
HÖHMAN, H.H. (1982) Economic Reform in the 1970s - policy with no alternative in A. Nove et al., op.cit. (see below)
KORNAI, J. (1971) Anti-equilibrium: On Economic Systems Theory and the Tasks of Research North-Holland, Amsterdam
MONTIAS, J.M. (1976) 'Principles of Resource Allocation and Real-Wage Determination for an Economy Maximising Capital Formation' in Thornton, op.cit. (see below)
NATO Colloquium (1980) Economic Reforms in Eastern Europe and Prospects for the 1980s Pergamon Press, Oxford
NISKANEN, W. (1968) 'Non-Market Decision-Making: the Peculiar Economics of Bureaucracy' American Economic Review Vol.58, pp.293-305
NISKANEN, W. (1973) Bureaucracy: Servant or Master? Hobart Paperback 5, Institute of Economic Affairs, London
NOVE, A. (1979) 'Planners Preferences, Priorities and Reforms' in A. Nove, Political Economy and Soviet Socialism Allen and Unwin, London
NOVE, A. (1983) The Economics of Feasible Socialism Allen and Unwin, London
NOVE, A. HÖHMAN, H., and SEIDENSTECHER, G. (1982) The East European Economies in the 1980s Butterworths, London

THORNTON, J. (1976) 'On Maximising Subject to a Planners' Feasibility Function' in Thornton, op.cit.

THORNTON, J. (ed)(1976) Economic Analysis of the Soviet-Type System Cambridge University Press

WANLESS, P.T. (1980) 'Economic Reform in Poland 1973-79' Soviet Studies Vol.32, No.1, pp.28-57

WARD, B. (1961) 'The Planners' Choice Variables' in B. Ward (ed), Value and Plan University of California Press, Berkley

WILLIAMSON, O.E. (1975) Markets vs. Hierarchies: Analysis and Anti-Trust Implications Free Press, New York

WOODALL, J. (1982) The Socialist Corporation and Technocratic Power Cambridge University Press

Chapter 3

TAXATION AND THE STEERING MECHANISM

TAXATION AND REFORM OF THE STEERING MECHANISM

The economic reforms discussed in Chapter 2 relate to the steering mechanism of the Plan sector, where the organisational units are financially autonomous enterprises/corporations. In reform of the steering mechanism, taxation plays a changed role by influencing the performance indicator and the incentive system, while continuing an unchanged role in the financing of the budgetary sector. In the steering mechanism, tax rates and regulations enter the response function as information, influencing the behaviour of producers by regulating the rewards for improved performance.

Typically, reforms introduce a new indicator of performance, in the form of a 'synthetic' indicator, usually some measure of profit. For the sake of generality, we shall call this indicator 'net profit', though other indicators have been tried. (For example, the Polish reforms of 1973-74 used value-added, and Yugoslavia also uses an indicator of value-added which is called 'net income'). Thus State corporations and enterprises become profit centres, and their financial autonomy is increased.

Typically, improvements in performance are measured by increases in net profit over the previous period, while a fall in net profit indicates a deterioration. (Some so-called reforms introduced plan targets for net profit, but these are not genuine reforms as we have defined them on pp. 23-25.)

The rewards for improved performance

are confirmed by making the corporation, rather than the State Budget, the beneficiary of net profit. Prior to reforms, it was generally the case that corporate profits, over and above those earmarked for self-financing of planned investment, were transferred to the State Budget. Thus, there was an effective marginal tax rate of 100% on profits. Improvements in net profit benefitted the State Budget, rather than corporate employees.

In reformed mechanisms, residual net profits benefit employees in two ways. Net profit is normally split into two parts. One part is used to pay bonuses and/or wage increases in recognition of improved performance. This part is credited to the corporation's wage fund, a book-keeping fund representing the corporation's right to disburse wage payments.

The remainder is credited to a so-called development fund, and may be used to fund small-scale investment at the discretion of management, over and above any planned investment. However, since investment represents a strategic, rather than an operating, decision, most investment remains centrally planned. These limited decentralised investment powers are of principal benefit in freeing head office from excessively detailed decision-making, and in enhancing managerial utility, power and prestige; in addition, a little extra investment enhances the corporation's productive capacity and future profitability.

The State can influence net profit left at the disposal of corporations through the system of business taxation. This provides an 'indirect' regulator of increases in wage income in the economy, and so influences the level of consumer purchasing power and aggregate demand. Though details of reforms vary, we may generalise by saying that four types of business tax are levied: firstly, turnover (sales) tax; secondly, wage fund tax; thirdly, capital charges; fourthly, profits tax. These taxes are discussed in more detail in subsequent chapters. (In addition, there are in practice a number of special taxes and subsidies, designed to cream off excess profits, or protect loss-makers).

The actual details of the synthetic performance indicator have varied over time and from country to country. In general, we can represent the net profit indicator symbolically as:

$$NP = (R - TC) - TT - WT - CT - PT$$

where NP = net profit
R = sales revenue (at market prices)
TC = total costs (including depreciation and bank interest payable).
TT = turnover tax
WT = wage-fund tax
CT = capital charge
PT = profits tax

The division of net profit can proceed in a variety of ways. The two main approaches are: (1) the (proportionate) growth of 'funds' (wage fund, and development fund), is related to the (proportionate) growth of the synthetic indicator; (2) the absolute change in the fund is related to the level of net profit.

In the first approach:

$$\frac{WF_1 - WF_0}{WF_0} = g\left[\frac{NP_1 - NP_0}{NP_0}\right]$$

$$\text{and } \frac{DF_1 - DF_0}{DF_0} = (1-g)\left[\frac{NP_1 - NP_0}{NP_0}\right]$$

where WF = wage fund
NP = net profit
DF = development fund
0.1 = time subscripts, relating to the previous and current period, respectively
g = a parameter, normally set by the central authorities ($0 < g < 1$)

In the second approach

$$WF_1 - WF_0 = k.NP$$

$$DF_1 - DF_0 = (1-k)NP$$

where k = a parameter, normally set by the central authorities ($0 < k < 1$)

Note that some portion of net profit is earmarked for investment, providing a basis for expansion of capital investment and economic growth. Note also that the actual division of profits observed in reform attempts occasionally differs from the simple two-way split. Poland, for example, has on occasion introduced a management bonus fund and an export incentives fund based on profits.

In looking at taxation in economic reforms, it is obvious to turn to questions of incidence and shifting in order to analyse the allocative effects of taxation. The economic theory of public finance emphasises that economic adjustments by those who bear the legal incidence of a tax can result in the tax burden being shifted to others, so that there is a difference between the legal and economic incidence of a tax (see Brown and Jackson,1982,p.228). This occurs, for example, in the case of sales tax, when a supplier raises the price of the taxed product. Legal incidence lies in the supplier, who is legally responsible for payment of the tax. But the tax burden is shifted to customers, who bear the economic incidence of the tax.

As Musgrave (1969, p.16) has pointed out, central control over prices considerably reduces the ability of producers in a socialist economy to shift the burden of a tax. We shall assume, therefore, that questions of incidence and shifting of taxes will not generally be a matter of producers' discretion, at least in the selectively decentralised mechanism, and we shall modify analysis of the economic effects of taxation to take account of this. Questions of shifting and incidence are more likely to be important in market socialism, when prices are freed from central control and are the object of managerial discretion.

A further issue of tax incidence is the difference between incidence in the short run (when the capital stock is fixed) and in the long run (when the capital stock is variable). In a socialist economy, under certain conditions, the size of the capital stock is given, at least from the viewpoint of managers and enterprises, and the capital stock can therefore be treated as fixed. The conditions under which this occurs are, firstly, that central planners retain control over investment, and, secondly, that investments which can be undertaken at managerial discretion have a negligible impact on the capital stock. In these conditions, questions of tax shifting can be confined to short-run analysis only. However, if decentralised, discretionary investment were to occur on any significant scale (as it does in Hungary, for example) the size of the capital stock would respond to taxation and questions of long-run tax shifting would arise. This response would occur partly because of taxation's effect on relative prices, but also because of the effect of taxation on enterprise net cash flows, which are a source of finance for decentralised investment. Taxation thus affects the budget constraint of enterprises.

One issue which might usefully be considered here is whether tax rates and other parameters of tax policy should be applied generally to all business organisations, or whether they should be individually addressed to a particular organisation. The case for 'addressed' tax rates is an echo of the command mechanism, with its individually addressed plan targets and directives. The apparent advantage would be a more precise control by the central planners, who could tailor the addressed tax rates to fit the particular circumstances of the addressee organisation. The disadvantages in terms of administrative cost, complexity and information requirements are obvious. Moreover, addressed parameters almost inevitably require central involvement in operating decisions, so sacrificing one of the advantages of decentralisation in terms of economising on the bounded rationality of central planners. (Addressed parameters would not be 'true' taxes, as we have defined them by the criteria outlined on pp.1-4 as they would lack generality).

By contrast, general tax parameters are simpler and cheaper to establish, imposing less stringent information requirements, and putting less of a strain on bounded rationality. Moreover, general considerations of economic efficiency would suggest that uniform tax rates are preferable to selective taxation, as uniform taxation imposes fewer distortions on economic choices. However, the decision to use addressed parameters and differentiated tax rates may be motivated by other considerations - for example, as emergency measures in response to temporarily adverse circumstances, or as a means of facilitating economic adjustments.

TAXATION IN 'COMMAND' AND 'REFORMED' MECHANISMS

This section attempts to compare the role of taxation in the command economy and in economic reforms. The picture of the role of taxation in a command economy draws heavily on experience of the Soviet Union, especially in the period before any attempt at economic reforms (as discussed by, say, Holzman, 1954). The Soviet Union has tended to remain a highly centralised 'command' economy, and its budgetary system tends to reflect this (see more recent works on the Soviet budgetary system, such as Birman, 1981, and Hutchings, 1982). The purpose of this section is, however, to make some general remarks about taxation in the command system in general rather than to outline the budgetary history of the Soviet Union in particular.

In the command system, there are primarily two sources of budget revenue: sales tax, and the profits of socialised enterprises. Sales tax revenue takes two forms: turnover tax, mainly on consumption goods and services, and tax collected in the course of operating price equalisation accounts in domestic and foreign trade. Budgetary revenue from the profits of socialised enterprises arises because the 'free remainder of profits' is transferred in its entirety to the State Budget. This 'free remainder' is what is left after deduction of turnover tax, and of profits earmarked in the Plan for self-financing of fixed investment, increased working capital, and any other purposes. The 'free remainder' is not treated as enterprise income, but as a kind of 'social dividend', used to finance budgetary expenditure. 'Free' profits are thus subject to 100% marginal taxation, and, as a result, 'free profits' play little or no role in motivation at enterprise level. However, total profits may influence motivation in those cases where bonuses are profit-related.

Turnover tax is a sales tax, primarily levied on consumption goods and services in the domestic market. Sales tax, as is well-known, drives a 'wedge' between buyer's price and seller's price in the market, and the resulting distortion of economic choice is often seen as reducing economic efficiency. Selective sales taxation is particularly likely to damage economic efficiency, since the amount of economic distortion is greater than in the case of uniform sales taxation. However, the economic distortions of the 'socialist' turnover tax were quite deliberate, part of a 'two-tier' pricing system, which set out to deliberately manipulate consumer demand to match planned supply. (See Chapter 5). As a result, turnover tax is an instrument of retail pricing policy, as well as a source of budgetary revenue.

A further source of revenue is the tax collected in the course of operating price equalisation accounts. Price equalisation accounts are designed to ensure that all traders buy or sell at the same State-administered price. A lucky deal which secures a selling price in excess of the administered price brings no gains to the astute trader, when price equalisation accounts are in operation; nor does a fortunate purchase at a price below the administered price. Instead, the price difference is creamed off as a tax to the State Budget. (At the same time, price subsidies are paid to guarantee prices for traders who sell at below administered price, or buy above it). Such policies are aimed at securing price stability.

In general, in the command economy, taxation is not seen as a major allocative force. Although taxation influences prices, the primary instrument for resource allocation is the Plan, implemented by directive commands to producers. Prices, especially consumer prices, have little or no impact on the size and structure of production. However, taxation influences relative retail prices, and the structure of consumer demand. Further, since turnover tax regulates the general level of consumer prices, turnover tax also regulates the general level of consumer purchasing power in the economy - which can be seen as a measure of stabilisation policy. However, consumer purchasing power can also be regulated by centralised wage policy, and by personal income taxation, either or both of which could replace turnover tax in this respect.

In the command economy, then, taxation's primary role is one of revenue raising to provide funds to finance the non-marketed output of the budgetary sector, and to finance the division of national income among different economic sectors. On the expenditure side, the Budget's role in division of national income takes a variety of forms; expenditures connected with price equalisation accounts and other price subsidies; payments of grants to finance investment in fixed assets and working capital; and grants to finance enterprise losses. Though these various subsidies and grants do, to some extent, undermine enterprise autonomy, enterprises are not completely reduced to the status of bureaus; they retain financial autonomy since they account for profit or loss, and they are not entirely, or even mainly grant-funded.

The changeover from a command economy to a reformed steering mechanism is accompanied by changes in taxation which are only one part of the overall reform package. The general trends of reform were outlined on pp. 23-28 ; in summary, they involve greater decentralisation of decision-making, a greater reliance on profit incentives, and a reduction in the extent and detail of administrative direction of the economy. Against this background, tax reforms are typically introduced, strengthening the role of 'indirect' steering mechanisms, relying on financial signals to motivate management and shape production. Turnover tax and other forms of sales tax are retained,but modified in some way, principally to reduce inefficiency and strengthen the influence of consumer preferences on production. (See Chapter 5). New taxes are introduced; though the details vary, we can generalise by characterising the new taxes by three typical instruments; capital charges, tax on the wage fund, and profits tax.

Capital charges are introduced to provide an opportunity cost of capital or target rate of return, as a stimulus to rationality and efficiency in the use of capital assets. It is argued that, where interest rates are administratively determined and normally set at a very low level, and where much investment is financed by profit retention and budgetary grant, then capital will normally be underpriced or even treated as a free good. In the absence of any domestic (financial) capital market, the underpricing of capital would lead to excessive capital investment, and underutilisation of the capital stock. Capital charges are discussed in more detail in Chapter 7.

A tax on the wage fund is introduced, mainly to increase the effective, or shadow, price of labour to the enterprise. The case for increasing the shadow price of labour is argued in Chapter 6, especially pp. 95-96. One of the stated objectives claimed in the course of economic reforms was the desire to induce economies in the use of labour, and encourage 'modernisation' and the use of labour-saving techniques in production. (As it happened, in most countries, capital charges and the tax on the wage fund were not normally introduced simultaneously. Capital charges belong to an 'early' reform movement of the 1960s, the tax on the wage-fund to later reforms in the 1970s. Thus, at different times, the relative prices of capital labour were altered in different directions by the new taxes.)

The introduction of a profits tax in some form went hand in hand with a change in the disposal of residual profit. Previously, the State Budget was the beneficiary of residual profit; reform made the enterprise the residual beneficiary, so that the introduction of profits tax actually represents a reduction in the tax rate on profits so long as the rate of profits tax is less than 100%. The purpose of the tax (discussed at greater length in Chapter 7) is to regulate the division of profit between the State and the enterprise.

The reform of steering mechanism thus alters the role of taxation in the following ways:

1. The influence of taxation on production decisions increases, as part of a general move to 'indirect economic management'.
2. New forms of taxation are introduced to serve new purposes.
3. Shadow prices for capital and labour are introduced, providing centrally determined parameters which are an input in decision-making at lower levels in reformed steering mechanism.
4. A new method of dividing profit between State and enterprise is introduced with the profits tax.

The third new role for taxation is especially interesting in the light of this study's attempts to apply Williamson's 'new institutional economics' to the Socialist economy. In the Central Planner's use of taxation as a means of shadow pricing, we have some parallel with the Head Office of an M-form corporation, which takes strategic decisions on target rate of return, rules of transfer pricing, etc, which are intended for implementation at divisional level.

FINANCIAL PLANNING

The most obvious steering mechanism for socialist economies (as they presently exist) is central planning. But since the socialist economy is a monetary economy, transactions involving flows of real goods and services also give rise to financial flows. Planning the flows of real goods and services also requires the planning of the necessary financial flows, so that economic actors have the purchasing power to carry out planned transactions (Central planning may also involve direct allocation of supply, compulsory deliveries etc, but even then, some payment is usually involved.)

The coordination of financial and physical planning constitutes a form of stabilisation policy, aimed at securing equilibrium in the economy by balancing planned flows of income and credit against planned output and expenditure. This is achieved by forecasting financial flows, and the resulting financial plans are the basis for monetary policy, credit policy and taxation policy.

What follows here is an outline of the main financial plans, based on the system of financial planning used in Poland in the 1970s (described by various Polish authors - e.g. Bolland, 1976; Czerwinska et al, 1978, Ch.III; Szyrocki, 1975). The Polish system does not seem to have changed much since the description given by Montias (1962), writing over 20 years ago. Financial planning elsewhere seems to conform reasonably well to the Polish example - see Garvy, 1966, Ch.4; Garvy 1977, pp.43-48; Berry, 1977, Vol.2, Ch.VIII; or Kuschpeta, 1978, pp.141-176; 230-232.

Macroeconomic financial plans can be

divided into two groups:

> A Synthetic balances are highly aggregated financial forecasts, outlining major financial and economic trends. They provide background material for more detailed operating plans, and for the coordination of plans.
>
> B Operating plans provide the basis for the implementation of monetary policy. Essentially, they plan the 'output' of the financial sector in terms of monetary emission, credits granted, and so on.

SYNTHETIC BALANCES

The three major synthetic balances are:

(a) the balance of national income and expenditure
(b) the State's financial balance
(c) the balance of household income and expenditure.

The Balance of National Income and Expenditure. This balance is based upon the national income accounts (see Table 3.1 on p.42) and provides a highly aggregated view of macroeconomic activity. The other two synthetic balances are closely related to this basic national income framework (based on the socialist concept of national income, i.e. net material product, rather than Western-style national income).

The State's Financial Balance. The State's financial balance sets out the financial resources available to the State, including the financial accumulation of socialised enterprises. Financial accumulation of socialised enterprises consists of profits plus taxes payable to the State Budget. This surplus value is appropriated (or can be appropriated) by the State to finance expenditure from the State Budget. This treatment of enterprise accumulation highlights the points made by Holzman (1954) and Bird (1964) drawing attention to the arbitrary distinction between taxation

TABLE 3.1 - The Balance of National Income and Expenditure

Income		Expenditure	
1 'Embodied' labour		3 Fund of production costs (excluding amortisation)	XX
(a) raw materials	XX		
(b) capital consumption	XX		
2 'Living' labour		4 Gross national income	
(a) wages	XX	(a) consumption	
(b) surplus value	XX	(i) individual	XX
		(ii) collective	XX
		(b) Gross real accumulation	
		(i) productive investment	XX
		(ii) non-productive investment	XX
		(iii) change in stocks	XX
	XX		XX

of enterprises and enterprise profits in a socialist economy. The treatment also confirms the view that, ultimately, profits of socialised enterprises represent resources of the State, not the enterprise.

The entries in the State's financial balance are closely related to the entries in the balance of national income and expenditure. The general concept of the State's financial balance is set out in Table 3.2 on p.43. To simplify, the foreign sector is ignored, and it is assumed that the economy is entirely socialised. The entries in Table 3.2 are cross-references to entries in Table 3.1 and in later tables. These cross-reference show how the financing of the State sector is an element of major financial flows in the economy (Owsiak, 1977, 1980).

The Balance of Household Income and Expenditure. The balance of household income and expenditure is outlined in Table 3.3 on p.44. This balance analyses financial flows in the consumer goods market, and is based on predictions of consumer incomes,

TABLE 3.2 - The State's Financial Balance

Income		Expenditure	
5 Financial accumulation of socialised enterprise (2b)	XX	9 Current expenditure of State Budget	
		(a) wages	XX
		(b) collective consumption (4aii)	XX
6 Amortisation (1b)	XX		
7 Taxes and duties on the household sector	XX	10 Gross financial accumulation	
		(a) productive investment (4bi)	XX
8 Growth of financial resources of households		(b) non-productive investment (4bii)	XX
(a) increase in savings	XX	(c) change in stocks (4biii)	XX
(b) increase in cash in circulation	XX	11 Increase in consumer credit	XX
		12 Increase in reserves of financial system	XX
	XX		XX

trends in personal savings, and changes in consumer indebtedness. (This last item is generally small, as consumer credit is rather underdeveloped in socialist countries.)

Table 3.3 is drawn up on the same assumptions as Tables 3.1 and 3.2, so that entries can be cross-referenced, showing the interrelationships between the consumer goods market, national income and expenditure, and State finance.

OPERATING PLANS

The main operating plans are:

(a) the State Budget
(b) the credit plan
(c) the cash plan

TABLE 3.3 - The Balance of Household Income and Expenditure

Income		Expenditure	
13 Wages paid by enterprises (2a)	XX	18 Individual consumption (4ai)	XX
14 Wages paid from State Budget (9a)	XX	19 Taxes and duties on the household sector (7)	XX
15 Transfer payments from State Budget	XX	20 Growth of financial resources of households (8)	XX
16 Increase in consumer credit(11)	XX		
17 Increase in reserves of financial system (12)	XX		
	XX		XX

TABLE 3.4 - The State Budget

Income		Expenditure	
21 Income from socialised enterprises		23 Current expenditure	
(a) taxes which form part of enterprise costs (part of 3)		(a) wages (9a)	XX
		(b) Transfer payments to households (15)	XX
		(c) collective consumption (4aiii)	XX
(b) turnover tax (part of 2b)	XX	24 Capital expenditure (part of 4b)	XX
(c) transfers of profits (part of 2b)	XX	25 Deposits with the National Bank of Poland (see Ch.4, pp.59-60)	XX
(d) amortisation payments (part of 1b)	XX		
22 Taxes and duties on the household sector (7)	XX		
	XX		XX

<u>The State Budget</u>. In terms of legal status, the State Budget is the most important financial plan. Preparation of the annual State Budget is closely linked to the preparation of the annual economic Plan, and, like the Plan, the State Budget is approved by the Parliament or National Assembly, and has the force of law.

The State Budget has two functions. It is not only the most important financial plan, it is also a plan of real economic activity. Its first function is financial, planning the flows of budgetary income which link together the State sector, socialised enterprises, and the household sector (and the residual private sector). The second function of the State Budget is to plan the provision of goods and services which are financed from the State Budget; this entails planning the activities of Budget-supported bureaus.

Table 3.4 gives a stylised outline of the State Budget. It is drawn up on the same assumptions as Table 3.1, 3.2 and 3.3, and shows how plans for budgetary income and expenditure can be traced back to the synthetic balances.

In spite of the legal supremacy of the State budget, it is sometimes argued that the State's financial balance is a more suitable planning tool. (See Owsiak 1977 and 1980; also Montias, 1962). The State's financial balance covers a wider range of financial flows, and gives a more comprehensive view of factors affecting equilibrium. The main objection advanced to using the State's financial balance as the major tool of planning is that it is too highly aggregated. The resulting lack of detail makes the State's financial balance unsuitable for planning the activities of budgetary units and establishments.

It is further argued that, in spite of the apparently wide coverage of the State's financial balance, there are some omissions which make it unsuitable as a main tool of planning. Transfer payments are excluded completely, but are of great importance in determining financial flows and financial equilibrium. This is because transfers to households influence consumer incomes, and, more importantly, transfers to enterprises to subsidise a wide range of goods and services are a very important feature of economic life. (In Table 3.4 price subsidies are included in 'collective consumption', entry 23c). A further exclusion from the State's financial balance arises because any part of enterprise taxation which is classified as part of enterprise costs (e.g. taxes on the wage-fund may be treated as labour costs) is not included in the financial accumulation of enterprises (2b, Table 3.1) and is therefore excluded from the State's income in the State's financial balance (see Table 3.2). As a result, the State Budget continues to be the main financial plan, with background provided by the State's financial balance.

TABLE 3.5 - The Credit Plan

Changes in liabilities		Changes in assets	
26 Changes in deposits by socialised enterprises	XX	31 Change in credit to socialised enterprise	
		(a) short-term credit	XX
27 Changes in savings deposits of households (8a)	XX	(b) investment credit	XX
28 Changes in deposits held by government departments and financial institutions	XX	32 Change in credit for personal consumption	XX
29 State deposits with the National Bank of Poland (25)	XX		
30 Change in cash in circulation	XX		
	XX		XX

Credit Plan. The credit plan is concerned with the assets and liabilities of the banking system, and the implications for the granting of credit. The credit plan is very closely related to the National Socio-Economic Plan, and directs the banking system on its responsibilities with regard to credit policy. Credit policy is primarily aimed at creating the financial conditions necessary to fulfil the Plan. A summary version of the credit plan is given in Table 3.5; it is drawn up on the same assumptions as preceding tables, and cross-referenced to them.

TABLE 3.6 - The Cash Plan

Withdrawals of cash from banking systems		Inflows of cash to banking systems	
33 Wages (2a)	XX	40 Sales of goods and services	XX
34 Transfer payments to households from State Budget (15)	XX	41 Taxes, duties and social security contributions	XX
35 Purchases of goods and services (a) by State sector	XX	42 Various other types of minor incomes	XX
(b) by socialised enterprises (1a)	XX	43 Repayments of credit	XX
36 New credit granted (related to 31 and 32)	XX	44 New deposits in household savings accounts	XX
37 Withdrawals from households' savings accounts	XX	45 Reduction in cash in tills at banks and post offices	XX
38 Growth of cash in tills at banks and post offices	XX	46 Growth of cash in circulation (see 30)	XX
39 Reduction in cash in circulation (see 30)	XX		
	XX		XX

Cash Plan. The cash plan is a means of planning monetary emissions consistent with maintaining market equilibrium. As far as the general public are concerned, the money supply consists almost wholly of cash since consumer credit is extremely limited, and personal cheque accounts are virtually unknown. As a result, the cash plan provides a powerful means of planning for consumer goods market equilibrium. The aim is to plan monetary emissions which just balance anticipated transactions. Coverage of the plan also extends to enterprises and the State sector, so the final plan is based upon an economy-wide analysis of the demand for cash, and the final plan instructs the monetary authorities on their monetary emission policy.

Table 3.6 on p.47 sets out a simplified version of the cash plan, drawn upon the same assumptions as preceding tables, and cross-referenced to them.

BALANCES IN PERSPECTIVE

Overall, these six balances provide a systematic framework for monetary and credit policy. Portes (1977) claims that the financial planning mechanism has generally succeeded in preventing the emergence of open inflation in the consumer goods markets in socialist countries, and that the system of financial planning is highly effective in this respect. On the other hand, Kornai, 1979, claims that financial plans for enterprises are very lax, impose no financial discipline or constraint, and are one of the factors leading to persistent excess demand and <u>suppressed</u> inflation in socialist economies. Kornai's contention is that financial plans are simply revised upwards to allow physical plans to be fulfilled if necessary.

SUMMARY

The reform of the steering mechanism involves changes in the style of economic management, and changes in the policy instruments. With the greater autonomy accorded to State corporations and enterprises, central planners use financial parameters to regulate the socialised economy, introducing new taxes to influence economic behaviour of producers through profit-related incentives. Theoretical considerations indicate that these new parameters should be general in nature, rather than individually addressed to each separate corporation or enterprise. The role of indirect management means that taxation requires new functions, and its role becomes qualitatively different, and more important, in a 'reformed' mechanism as contrasted with a 'command' mechanism. In both mechanisms, however, taxation is important in financial planning, since taxes influence flows of funds and purchasing power in the economy.

REFERENCES

BERRY, L.V. (1977) Planning a Socialist Economy (2 vols) Progress Publishers, Moscow

BIRMAN, I. (1981) Secret Incomes of the Soviet State Budget Martinus Nijhoff Publisher, The Hague, Boston and London

BOLLAND, S. (1976) Introduction to Financial Science (Polish) State Economic Publishers, Warsaw

BROWN, C.V. and JACKSON, P.M. (1982) Public Sector Economics, (2nd ed.) Martin Robertson, Oxford

CZERWINSKA, E. et al. (1978) Finance - a Textbook for Higher Education in Economics (Polish) State Scientific Publishers, Warsaw

GARVY, G. (1966) Money, Banking and Credit in Eastern Europe Federal Reserve Bank of New York

GARVY, G. (1977) Money, Financial Flows and Credit in the Soviet Union Ballinger, Cambridge, Mass.

HOLZMAN, F.D. (1954) Soviet Taxation Harvard University Press, Cambridge, Mass.

HUTCHINGS, R. (1983) The Soviet Budget Macmillan, London

KORNAI, J. (1979) 'Resource-constrained vs Demand-constrained Systems' Econometrica Vol.47, No.4, pp.801-819

KUSCHPETA, O. (1978) The Banking and Credit System of the USSR Martinus Nijhoff, Leiden and London

MONTIAS, J.M. (1962) Central Planning in Poland Yale University Press,New Haven and London

MUSGRAVE, R.A. (1969) Fiscal Systems Yale University Press, New Haven and London

OWSIAK, S. (1977) 'The State's Financial Balance

in the Theory and Practice of Planning' (Polish) Finanse No.6, June, pp.1-12

OWSIAK, S. (1980) The State's Financial Balance: Theory and Practice of Planning (Polish)State Economic Publishers, Warsaw

PORTES, R. (1977) 'The Control of Inflation: Lessons from East European Experience' Economica Vol.44, No.174, pp.109-130

SZYROCKI, J. (1975) Financial Policy in the People's Republic of Poland (Polish) Polish Economic Society, Katowice

Chapter 4

TAXATION AND THE STATE BUDGET

BUDGETARY REVENUES

This section presents some illustrative budgetary data for 'socialist' countries in the European bloc. The data relate to size and type of incomes of the State budget. The size of a country's budgetary income is often taken as indicative of the importance of the State Budget in the national economy, and as an indicator of the size of the State (or public) sector. Furthermore, the structure of budgetary income and the type of instrument used to raise revenue are interesting, from the point of view of public (State) finance.

The budgetary data are taken mainly from statistical yearbooks published by the country concerned, and are for budgetary outturn - i.e. for realised revenue, not the projected revenues of the annual budgetary law. The data present a number of problems, which must be borne in mind when making interpretations or comparisons.

Firstly, each country uses a somewhat different presentation, and there is considerable variation in the amount of detail provided and the terminology used. In describing income items, the terms 'tax' 'levy' and 'payment' are often used interchangeably, as are 'duties' 'fees' and 'charges'. As a result, one cannot always be certain which items are actually taxes as we defined them on pp. 1-4.

Secondly, the classification of budgetary revenues differ from country to country, and over time. Classifications are revised at irregular intervals, often because there have been changes in the budgetary system. Thus there is some lack of comparability in data, both between countries and over time.

Thirdly, for some countries, there are 'gaps' in the presentation of budgetary income, so that the various types of incomes do not sum to total income reported. (These 'gaps' are particularly well known with regard to the Soviet Union - see Birman, 1981). Where 'gaps' have been found in the data presented in this chapter, their existence has been noted.

Fourthly, the conventional wisdom has it that the socialist State Budget is a consolidated budget, embracing all levels of central and local government. However, this is not true of Yugoslavia, or of Czechoslovakia. As Jurkovicz (1982-83) has recently pointed out, there is virtually no aggregate budgetary data available for Yugoslavia; available data relate mainly to the 'income' (source unspecified) of different types of 'social organisation'. Thus no information is presented for Yugoslavia. Czechoslovakia's main information about budgetary income (by type of income) comes in the form of separate budgets for central and local government, though some fragmentary consolidated data is also given. There seems to be no published statistical data on the State Budget in Bulgaria, at least, not in the annual statistical yearbook.

Data on budgetary incomes and type of income for Czechoslovakia, East Germany, Hungary, Poland, Romania and the USSR are given in Tables 4.1 through 4.6. In general, the data are taken more or less straight from the published statistical yearbooks, with some additional detail for the 1980 figures for the USSR which is taken from a specialised book of budgetary statistics, published every five years or so. However, in some cases, minor income items have been aggregated to reduce the size of the tables, and some additional sub-totals inserted for the sake of clarity. The entries for 'unidentified income' are computed by the author, and relate to the 'gaps' in data mentioned above.

The data pertain to the latest available years, which depends upon timeliness of data publication and dissemination. In some areas, data for two recent years are presented. In the case of Poland, there were some marked changes in budget structure in 1982, so data for 1981 are also shown. For the Soviet Union, more detail is available for 1980 than 1982, so figures for both years are given. Data for other countries are either for 1981 or 1982. It was not felt necessary to restrict the data to the same year for each country, as the purpose of providing the data is to illustrate certain points about the State Budget, rather than to be rigorously analytical.

Czechoslovakia

TABLE 4.1 Czechoslovakia: Income of State (Central Government) Budget and People's Council's Budgets, 1981

SECTION I Income of State Budget & People's Councils (1981)

	Million Crowns	% of Income
Income from socialised economy	256,090	82.1
Taxes and charges on the population	42,316	13.6
Other income	13,162	4.2
Total Income	311,568	100.0
of which:		
turnover tax	82,483	26.5
agricultural taxes	3,687	1.2
income tax	1,779	0.6
tax (on the population)	40,059	12.9
other taxes and charges	1,335	0.4
local taxes	609	0.2
	129,952	

SECTION II Income of State Budget (1981)

	Million Crowns	% of Income
Turnover tax	75,564	28.5
Income from socialised enterprises	123,978	46.8
Income from banking and insurance organisations	15,590	5.9

continued

TABLE 4.1, SECTION II (continued)

	Million Crowns	% of Income
Income from budget supported organisations	4,160	1.6
Financial income	41,559	15.7
Social insurance contributions	539	0.2
Other income	3,644	1.4
Total identified income	265,034	*
Unidentified income	-	-
Total reported income	265,034	*

SECTION III Income of People's Councils (1981)

	Million Crowns	% of Income
Income from socialised enterprises	11,196	10.8
Income from banking and insurance organisations	281	0.3
Taxes and charges	15,085	14.6
Income from budget-supported organisations	5,425	5.2
Social security contribution	3,617	3.5
Subsidies from State Budget	29,334	28.3
Subventions from State Budget	27,788	26.8
Other income	10,930	10.5
Total identified income	103,656	100.0
Unidentified income	-	-
Total reported income	103,656	100.0

* Note
Percentages sum to more than 100% due to rounding errors.

Section I of Table 4.1 gives what consolidated budgetary data are available. The data indicate the heavy importance of the socialised economy in providing over 80% of revenue for the State Budget, and relative unimportance of the household sector ('population'). The breakdown of total income by type of budgetary instrument is incomplete, but indicates that turnover tax is very prominent in providing budgetary revenue.

Confusingly, Czechoslovakia calls its central government budget the 'State Budget', a term which elsewhere is applied to the consolidated central/local budget. Section II shows the central government budget. Income from socialised enterprises is the single most important source of central government revenue. There are no apparent gaps in the breakdown of revenue, but the entry for 'financial income' is rather mysterious. The Czech term 'financni' can also be translated as 'from the Treasury' or 'from the Exchequer'; but what this 'financial' or 'Exchequer' income might be is obscure. It probably does not represent income from the financial sector, as there is a separate entry for banking and insurance. It seems unlikely to represent income from fees and charges paid to the Exchequer/Treasury, because of its size. Possibly it represents an attempt to 'balance the books' by drawing on previously accumulated budgetary surpluses - an expedient also used by Poland (see below). In this case, the Czech State Budget is probably in deficit (see pp.67, and 58-60).

Section III of this table relates to income of local government. The local government sector's income is substantial, but over half of it is in the form of grants from central government. However, local government has an income in its own right, mostly representing 'ear-marked' revenues rather than independent tax-raising powers. In 1981, local governments' own income amounted to over 46 billion crowns, or about 14% of total budgetary revenue. Although the other countries presented here also have separate local and central budgets, they give a more complete consolidated budget than is the case for Czechoslovakia. For Czechoslovakia it is necessary to look at the separate local and central budgets to get a complete picture. This is not the case for the other five countries.

German Democratic Republic

The GDR publishes long and very detailed

TABLE 4.2 Budgetary Income, GDR, 1981

	Million Marks	% of Income
Income from socialised corporations and enterprises:		
Capital charges	19,769	11.8
Taxes on net profit	42,082	25.0
Turnover tax	37,702	22.5
Levies on the banking system	6,752	4.0
Taxes on agriculture	1,458	0.9
Taxes on workers' cooperatives	3,344	2.0
Total socialised sector	111,107	66.4
Taxes on the self-employed and private businesses	3,173	1.9
Income tax on workers and employees	7,217	4.3
Social security contributions	15,670	9.4
(of which: employers' contributions	(8,918)	(5.3)
employees' contributions)	(6,752)	(4.0)
Local authority taxes	562	0.3
Miscellaneous fees, charges and other income	10,735	6.4
Total identified income	148,464	88.7*
Unidentified income	19,003	11.3
Total income	167,467	100.0

* Note

Percentage calculated as $\frac{148,458}{167,467} \times 100$.

The figure in the table exceeds the total of percentages for individual items, due to rounding errors.

statistics on budgetary income by type of income, and these data are the basis for Table 4.2. Unfortunately almost all of the detail given relates to details of fees and charges levied; since these only account for about 6½% of total revenue, they have been condensed to a single entry. The data confirm the impression of the great importance of the socialist economy in generating revenue. However, the breakdown of budgetary income accounts for only 88.6% of income; the remaining 11.4% is unaccounted for.

Hungary

TABLE 4.3 Hungary, State Budget, 1982

	Billion florints	% of Income
Payments by socialised enterprises and corporations	256.2	52.7
Payments by agricultural cooperatives	15.2	3.1
Turnover taxes on consumption goods	71.8	14.8
Total socialist sector	343.2	70.6
Payments by population	11.4	2.4
Social security payments	74.5	15.3
Miscellaneous fees, charges, and other income	56.7	11.7
Total identified income	485.8	100.0
Unidentified income	-	-
Total income per official Budget statistics	485.8	100.0

Hungary has recently greatly reduced its statistical coverage of the budgetary sector and budgetary income, and Table 4.3 represents all that is currently available. However, there are no obvious gaps in the data, although, obviously, such a highly aggregated classification can conceal a great deal.

Poland

Poland provides considerable detail on

TABLE 4.4 State Budget of Poland, 1981 and 1982

	1981		1982	
	Billion zlotys	%	Billion zlotys	%
Turnover tax	368.1	27.6	626.0	26.7
Payments from profit	137.7	10.3	141.6	6.0
Capital charges on fixed assets	32.8	2.5	-	-
Favourable budgetary differences	66.0	4.9	14.4	0.6
Once-and-for-all stabilisation tax	-	-	94.8	4.1
Income tax (on cooperatives)	28.8	2.2	791.5	33.8
Amortisation payments	21.6	1.6	41.1	1.8
Differences from reducing prices of goods	10.1	0.8	47.6	2.0
Levy on wage fund	73.7	5.5	2.0	0.1
Tax on wage fund	77.5	5.8	206.3	8.8
Tax on enterprise funds and bonus funds	38.7	2.9	-0.1	-
Tax on immoveable property of units of socialised economy	6.0	0.5	34.8	1.5
Rural taxes and charges on socialised industry	1.2	0.1	0.3	-
Social insurance contributions from socialised industry	78.3	5.9	97.6	4.2
Total from socialised industry	940.5	70.5	2097.9	89.6
Miscellaneous fees, charges and other incomes	9.4	0.7	12.3	0.5
Taxes and charges on the non-socialised economy	15.2	1.1	27.8	1.2
Taxes and charges on the population	18.8	1.4	20.8	0.9
Total identified income	983.9	73.7	2158.7	92.2
Income from return of budgetary deposits	155.6	11.7	4.3	0.2
Unidentified income	195.1	14.6	177.9	7.6
Total reported income	1334.6	100.0	2341.0	100.0

budgetary finance, and the breakdown of income from the socialised sector by type of instrument is particularly detailed. Items represented elsewhere by one category have several categories here. Because of the detail and terminology involved, some explanation is in order.

Sales tax is represented by turnover tax, and by 'favourable budgetary differences', which are a tax associated with the operation of price equalisation accounts (See Chapter 5). Taxes and payments from profit have several entries: payments from profit, income tax on cooperatives, amortisation payments (on fixed assets financed by budgetary grant), and tax on enterprise funds and bonus funds (these funds are based, at least in part, on net profit). Capital charges in Poland were levied on fixed assets only. They were abolished in 1982,and replaced by a real estate tax ('tax on immoveable property of units of socialised economy'). Up until 1982 Poland had two wage fund taxes; one (the 'levy') was introduced in the course of the economic reforms of 1973, and survived for several years after the reforms had been abandoned. The other (the 'tax') was introduced to replace revenue lost when personal income tax was largely phased out (1972-76). In addition, Poland levies social insurance contributions, as part of the social security system. The entry for 'differences from reducing prices of goods' probably refers to income exacted from economic units for imposing unauthorised price increases. If such practices are detected by external auditors, the excess profit plus a penalty payment is transferred to the State Budget. The once-and-for-all stabilisation tax is a temporary tax surcharge, levied at a time of a rising budget deficit, rapid inflation, and falling output. The wisdom of such a move may appear somewhat questionable.

Poland has also taken to including in budgetary income a figure for 'return of budget deposits with the National Bank of Poland'. In the 1970s, when the Polish budget was in surplus, the surplus was deposited with the National Bank. These past 'savings' are now being drawn on in an attempt to balance the books. However, there is still a 'gap' between revealed sources of income and the total income reported. The 'gap' was reduced sharply between 1981 and 1982, by the stabilisation tax; by the increased revenue from turnover tax (up 70% as retail prices increased sharply); and by an astounding leap in revenue from income tax from cooperatives.

Romania

TABLE 4.5 Romania, State Budget, 1981

	Billion Lei	% of Income
Income from socialist economy:		
Payments from profits of State economy units	82.0	29.3
Tax on value of net product	59.1	21.1
Turnover tax	34.9	12.5
Tax on wages fund	36.7	13.1
Other income from socialist economy	20.8	7.4
Total income from socialist economy	233.5	83.3
Agricultural tax	0.9	0.3
Social insurance contributions	34.7	12.4
Taxes on the population	3.2	1.1
Miscellaneous income	8.0	2.9
Total identified income	280.3	*
Unidentified income	-	-
Total income	280.3	*

* Note
Percentages do not sum to 100% due to rounding errors.

Romania, like Hungary, gives very little in the way of a detailed breakdown of budgetary figures by type of income. What information there is is given in Table 4.5. As in the Hungarian case, there are no obvious gaps in the data.

USSR

TABLE 4.6 State Budget of the USSR, 1980 and 1982

	1981 Billion roubles	1981 %	1982 Billion roubles	1982 %
Turnover tax	94.1	31.1	100.6	28.5
Payments by State enterprises & corporations out of profits	89.9	29.7	102.4	29.0
of which: Capital charges	29.2	9.6	28.0	7.9
Transfers of free remainder of profits	44.0	14.3	46.3	13.1
Fixed (rent) payments	0.4	0.1	5.2	1.5
Deductions from profit and other payments	16.2	5.4	19.7	5.6
Income tax from co-operatives, agricultural cooperatives and enterprises of social organisations	1.7	0.6	1.9	0.5
Total socialised sector	185.7	61.3	204.9	58.0
State lottery - loans sold to population	0.6	0.2	1.0	0.3
State lottery - revenue	0.3	0.1	n.a.	-
Direct taxes from the population	24.5	8.1	26.6	7.5
State social insurance funds	14.2	4.7	22.3	6.3
Stumpage charges	0.5	0.2	n.a.	-
Total identified income	225.8	74.6	254.8	72.2
Unidentified income	76.9	25.4	98.2	27.8
Total reported inome	302.7	100.0	353.0	100.0

Published statistical data on budgetary income for the USSR are known to be incomplete, although Birman, 1981, has, by patient detective work, succeeded in estimating some of the missing sources, and has narrowed the 'gap' considerably. However, the statistical yearbooks and the specialised budget 'yearbook' give only the detail given in Table 4.6, though the specialised budget publication gives a breakdown of taxes on the population for 1980:

income tax 23.0 billion roubles; agricultural tax 0.3 billion roubles; tax on single persons and small families (levied as a pronatalist policy in 'European' republics) 1.3 billion roubles. The entry for 'stumpage charges' refers to income from the forestry industry, presumably based on the number of trees felled.

OVERVIEW AND COMPARISON OF BUDGETARY REVENUES

TABLE 4.7 Budgetary revenue as a percentage of national income (net material product).

Czechoslovakia, 1981	66%
German Democratic Republic, 1981	86%
Hungary 1982	70%
Poland 1981	62%
Romania 1981	51%
USSR 1980	66%

Table 4.7 illustrates the relationship between total reported budgetary revenue, and national income (on a net material product basis). The table apparently shows that a high proportion of national income ends up being channelled through the budget. However, the proportion varies, ranging from a low of 51% for Romania, to a high of 86% for GDR. It should be recalled, of course, that the net material product basis for measuring national income produces a lower figure than would be produced by a 'Western' income-expenditure approach. The usual rule of thumb is that net material product figures are about 20% smaller than those calculated by Western conventions. Further, the figures are affected by the 'gaps' in the revenue statistics, which may mean that budgetary income is overstated for GDR, Poland and USSR.

Within the overall total of budgetary income, budgetary structure varies. In Chapter 3, we identified certain forms of income as being typical of a 'command economy' (turnover tax and other sales taxes, and payments from profit), while we characterised other instruments as new instruments associated with economic reforms (profits tax, capital charges, and wage-fund tax). However, it is not always possible to identify these 'new' taxes of economic reform from the budgetary statistics, for two reasons. Firstly, the budget classification does not always identify revenue from these new taxes. Secondly, not all reform attempts were precisely the same, and not all the tax systems of 'reforming' countries had taxes precisely conforming to the stereotypes outlined on pp. 23-28. (Poland's reforms of 1973-75, for example, had no tax on the synthetic indicator of performance, value-added, but did involve capital charges and wage-fund tax.)

Furthermore, it is not always possible to say whether or not a country is a command economy or a reformed system on the basis of taxes levied. Taxes introduced as part of one reform attempt are not always abolished if (when) the reforms fail, and the steering mechanism reverts to a command system.

Looking over our six countries, we find that the bulk of revenue is raised from the socialised sector. Using a somewhat free translation, we can say that 'business taxation' is more important than 'personal' taxation. However, there are differences in presentation of data. Czechoslovakia and Poland both include social insurance contributions in budgetary income from the socialised sector; the other countries present them separately. If we include social insurance contributions in income from the socialised sector, then we can calculate that the proportion of budgetary income raised from the socialised sector ranges from about 70%, to over 95% in the case of Romania. Without social insurance contributions, the proportion ranges from about 60% to over 80%. However, the proportions so calculated are distorted by considerable gaps in data for GDR, Poland and USSR. The gaps are considerable in size, but vary in extent. No such gaps are identifiable for Czechoslovakia, Hungary or Romania.

Turnover tax, previously regarded as a mainstay of budgetary revenue, now appears to account for less than 30% of total budgetary revenue; indeed, the proportion is considerably lower in Hungary (less than 15%) and Romania (around 12%). Of the budgetary revenue raised from the socialised sector, turnover tax contributes from around 15% (Romania) up to 50%

(USSR). (All these proportions are, of course, subject to error, due to the incompleteness of the data).

Payments from profit generate another substantial slice of total budgetary income. Defining 'payments from profit' is itself tricky, as countries differ in the way budget statistics are classified, and it can be hard to decide whether e.g. capital charges are an element of costs or whether they are paid out of profit. In order to reach a workable definition, the author decided to exclude capital charges, taxes on the wage fund, turnover tax and social security contributions. Payments from profit thus include: transfer of profit, either by wholesale transfer (USSR) or by tax (GDR), taxes on profit-related items (net product in Romania, enterprise and bonus funds in Poland); income tax on cooperatives; amortisation payments (Poland); and levies on the banking sector. The resultant calculations seem to indicate that the importance of such payments ranges from 20% or less (Poland and USSR) to more than 50% (Hungary). This variation may be partly due to the differences in classification and structure of taxes, but may also reflect the differing profitability of industry in the different countries. (Differences in profitability are only weakly related to efficiency, however).

Assessing the revenue significance of new taxes associated with economic reforms is very difficult. For capital charges, only GDR, USSR and Poland report separate figures, and Poland abolished its capital charge in 1982. In GDR, capital charges generated about 12% of budgetary revenue, in Poland only 2½%, in USSR almost 10%. Wage fund tax associated with economic reforms is reported by Poland and Romania, but the Polish situation is confused by the existence of a second wage fund tax. The two together seem to have generated about 9-11% of revenue, while in Romania the proportion was apparently higher - about 13%. Only two countries report revenue for anything like a tax on net profit - GDR, and Romania (tax on net product). The revenue contribution is about 25% in GDR, 21% for Romania. All in all, the new taxes could be substantial revenue-raisers, but the deficiencies in statistical presentation make it difficult to attach any very precise quantitative significance.

Social insurance contributions are reported for every country. Their importance varies. In Czechoslovakia, they provide about 1½% of total (consolidated) budgetary revenue, which is very low compared to the other countries. Figures range from 4-6% in Poland and USSR, up to over 15% in Hungary.

The importance of direct personal taxation varies. The term 'taxes on the population' is usually interpreted to mean direct taxes. Czechoslovakia raises over 12% of revenue by means of 'tax' on the population, GDR raises about 4% from income tax on workers and employees, with a further 2% raised by taxing private businesses. Hungary raises only 2.4% from payments by population. Poland gets around 2% of revenue from taxes on the population and taxes on the private sector, Romania apparently only about 1%. In the USSR direct taxes account for about 7-8% of revenue. The low figure for Poland and Romania is explained by the fact that personal income tax has largely been abolished in those countries.

Overall, we see that in the real world, budgetary instruments are more varied, and more complex than the simple reform stereotype suggests. The overall structure of budgets varies from country to country, as does the completeness and reliability of data.

THE BALANCE OF THE BUDGET

In the public finance of 'capitalist' countries, the balance of the budget is often seen as a key policy instrument. In Keynesian theory, the deficit or surplus of the budget is an instrument of stabilisation policy, designed to secure full employment, and/or avoid inflationary pressure. More recently, especially in Britain, attention has focussed on reducing the overall deficit of the State sector (the Public Sector Borrowing Requirement) in order to reduce inflationary pressure in the economy.

However, a rather different view is taken of the socialist State Budget. First of all, it is argued, central planning takes care of the problem of full employment, so a budget deficit is unnecessary. (Kaleta, 1977, p.43). Secondly, it is often argued that not only is the State Budget in overall balance, so too are the budgets of each level of administration - according to Kaleta (op. cit. p.46), this is so even down to parish level. Thirdly, it is alleged that if an unbalanced budget is required, a socialist economy requires a surplus. On the one hand, a surplus helps to neutralise inflationary pressure resulting from expansion of bank credit in the course of economic growth and development (Czerwinska et al, 1975, p.220). On the other hand, Gajl (1974, pp.404-405), argues that the budget surplus is transferred to the banking system, to finance investment expenditures through interest-bearing bank credit. Thus the surplus is an element in the redistribution of national income through the State Budget.

Typically, the socialist economies of the Soviet Union and Eastern Europe report budget surpluses, though Hungary reports deficits more regularly than most. According to Jurkovicz (1982/83, p.22), budget balance is seen as an end in itself in Yugoslavia, with no account taken of whether a deficit or surplus might be required to offset economic fluctuations in the rest of the economy. Birman (1981, p.10) reports that Soviet authors take the absence of a budget deficit as evidence of some particular advantage of the Soviet financial system. However Czerwinska et al (1978, p.219-20) acknowledge that overall market equilibrium may require an unbalanced budget, and that this may require a deficit. Gajl (1974, p.402) states that a socialist State is not free from the problem of deficit financing and public indebtedness, but claims that the socialist State's method of dealing with the problem takes different forms from deficit financing in capitalist countries. She specifically mentions forced loans from the population, used in the Soviet Union from 1922 onwards, and by most of the socialist countries in the 1950s. She also refers to financing by monetary emission in Bulgaria and Poland after World War II. Finally she refers to the practice of transferring free reserves of banking and insurance institutions to the State Budget and treating these as 'budgetary income', a practice she claims is confined to the Soviet Union and Poland. Birman (1981) claims that the banking system in the Soviet Union systematically finances a budget deficit by increasing the money supply. Birman bases this conclusion on the observed incomplete breakdown of budgetary income in official statistics of the USSR, and argues that the gap must be filled by monetary emission - he claims there can be no other explanation, and that the monetary emission makes up for the 'missing' budget revenue. Similar explanations could be expounded for the gaps in budgetary income for GDR and Poland.

The Polish authorities have publicly acknowledge that there is a deficit on the State Budget; in 1980, the newspaper Zycie Gospodarcze (1980, No.50, p.5) reported a projected budget deficit of 100 billion zlotys for 1981. In the event, the statistical yearbook reported a deficit of 131 billion slotys, with expenditure of 1,465.6 billion zlotys, income 1,344.5 billion zlotys. However, that income included 155.6 billion zlotys described as 'return of deposits with National Bank of Poland' - representing past budget surpluses. Since these can hardly be counted as current income, this indicates a budget deficit of 286.6 billion zlotys, or about 20% of expenditure. In 1982, a surplus was reported: expenditure 2,166.4 billion zlotys, income 2,345.3 of which only 4.3 billion zlotys represented 'return of deposits'.

In section 4.1 we drew attention to the possibility of Czechoslovakia's income in the form of financial income might also represent a budget deficit - of the order of 13% of expenditure.

If Birman is correct in claiming that the Soviet Union conceals a budget deficit, and if the official statistics discussed above also attempt to conceal or understate a budget deficit, it is difficult to know why such concealment is considered necessary. Birman implies that a budget deficit would be regarded as a sign of weakness, but this factor does not seem to inhibit the Hungarians, for their central statistical office publishes budget deficits: 0.9% of expenditure in 1975 0.8 in 1979, 2.2% in 1980, 2.0% in 1981, 2.4% in 1982. However these deficits are very small, and probably could be accounted for by errors in budget forecasting. Birman claims that the Soviet Union's budget deficit has been growing since 1966, and reached 9% of expenditure by 1978 (1981 pp.11, 110-111). Such a substantial deficit might well be seen as a more serious matter.

However, it is difficult to see why particularly great importance should be attached to having a balance/surplus on the State Budget. A balanced budget is not necessarily the key to equilibrium in the economy. A simple Keynesian framework tells us that overall equilibrium in national income may well require a budget deficit if, ex ante, savings in the economy exceed investment, or if there is a foreign trade deficit.

Furthermore, consider the injections-withdrawal approach to macroeconomic equilibrium which is used in many undergraduate text-books. Suppose the withdrawals from the circular flow of income are: taxation (T), savings (S) and imports (M), while injections into the circular flow are government expenditure on goods and services (G), investment (I) and exports (X). Macroeconomic equilibrium requires that injections equal withdrawals, or

$$(G+I+X) - (T+S+M)$$

Alternatively

$$(G-T) + (I-S) + (X-M) = 0$$

If $X=M$, and $I<S$, then we must have $G>T$ in equilibrium, which implies a budget deficit. On the other hand, if $I=S$, and $X<M$, so that there is a foreign trade deficit, equilibrium requires that $G>T$, so that there is a budget deficit. The State Budget is not the only financial plan. The aim of financial planning is to secure a balance between monetary expansion and the growth of goods and services for sale. In terms of the financial planning system of the previous chapter, a budget deficit reduces State deposits with the central bank, which, other things being equal, would reduce bank liabilities and assets, reducing the amount of credit which could be offered by the banking system. However, if deposits by enterprises and/or households were growing, this could offset the budget deficit. The danger might be that the credit plan would be balanced by excessive monetary expansion, with inflationary consequences. This might well explain the concern for a balanced budget: it reflects a desire for non-inflationary financing of bank credit. However, concealing the true deficit would not prevent any adverse consequences of deficit financing.

BUREAUS AND PARABUDGETS

Supply of goods and services within the budgetary sector is entrusted to a set of budgetary institutions or 'bureaus' which are financed by grant from the State Budget, and whose income (if any) is returned to the State Budget.

Some socialist countries make a distinction between bureaus which are expected to charge for their services, and those which are not. In Poland, for example, the former are called 'budgetary establishments', the latter 'budgetary units'.

Budgetary units are found in all socialist countries, and in capitalist economies like Britain and USA as well. Budgetary units supply goods free of charge, and are financed entirely from State revenues. They include such institutions as schools, colleges, hospitals and military establishments. This form would seem appropriate whenever it is infeasible or undesirable to charge a price for the goods, either because the goods are true 'public goods' (Musgrave, 1959, Ch.1) and exclusion is infeasible or because they are 'merit' goods, and charging is ruled out on political or ethical grounds. In theory, budgetary establishments are encouraged to raise additional funds by various sidelines wherever possible - for example, by sales of produce from agricultural colleges, renting out empty sheds or offices, or fattening pigs on hospital left-overs.

Budgetary establishments are occasionally claimed as particularly well-developed in Poland, as compared to other socialist economies in Eastern Europe (for example, by Kaleta, 1977, p.83). This form could be used, in principle, whenever it is desirable and feasible to apply the exclusion principle by charging for the product. However, the price charged does not usually cover the full cost, and the resulting deficit is covered from the State Budget. To try to encourage efficiency in spite of the subsidy, budgetary establishments are usually expected to cover a certain proportion of their costs out of revenue. (In Poland, this proportion is 60%). Various cultural activities, such as theatres, fall into this category; other activities organised in this form are very diverse, and include kindergartens and creches, youth clubs, sports centres, the services of the weights and measures inspectorate, and analytical laboratories.

In the socialist economies of Eastern Europe, a further feature of State financing is the existence of 'parabudgets'. These are extra-budgetary funds, set up to finance particular activities. (Swatler, 1979, pp.111-121; Owsiak, 1974). The funds are drawn partly from the State Budget and partly from voluntary contributions from the general public. Parabudgets are special purpose funds, set up to attract contributions by earmarking the use of those funds for especially worthy purposes. Their importance varies from country to country, but they are especially highly developed in Poland. They differ greatly in their functions. Some, connected with aspects of health care, agriculture or housing, are permanent institutions. Others set up for strictly short-term purposes, such as the building of a new children's hospital in Warsaw, or rebuilding the Royal Castle in Warsaw. The income and expenditure of parabudgets are not consolidated into the State Budget, and each fund is administered separately. The aim of the funds is to add some elasticity to budgetary revenues by using the goodwill of the general public as a basis for fund-raising, rather than the compulsion of taxation. (Polish appeals are sometimes extended abroad, to draw on the goodwill of the expatriate community.) However, as each fund is administered separately, costs of administration and collection are high. The extent to which contributions from the domestic population are genuinely voluntary is debatable; in the case of certain funds in Poland, workers are expected to contribute as a matter of course.

Special purpose funds may also be set up out of general budgetary revenue. Sometimes taxes are especially earmarked for this purpose. A certain proportion of the wage fund tax in Poland is earmarked for the social insurance fund, while part of the land tax is used to finance the agricultural development fund. Such earmarking has a certain propoganda value, as well as being a means of enforcing budgetary discipline and control.

SUMMARY

This chapter has explored the role of taxation in the State Budget by means of scrutiny of some illustrative budgetary statistics. The statistics suggested that the revenue structure of six representative countries varied considerably, but the statistics themselves are defective, in that the classification of budgetary items varies, terminology differs, and the completeness of the statistical breakdown of revenue varies from country to country. The picture is further confused by the possibility that the statistics are manipulated to conceal the true extent of a budget deficit, and by the existence of extra-budgetary financing for certain State activities.

REFERENCES

BIRMAN, I. (1981) Secret Incomes of the Soviet State Budget Martinus Nijhoff Publisher, The Hague, Boston and London

CZERWINSKA, E. et al (1978), Finance - a Textbook for Higher Education in Economics (Polish) State Scientific Publishers, Warsaw

GAJL, N. (1974) The Budget and the State Treasury (Polish) State Economic Publishers, Warsaw

HUTCHINGS, R.C. (1983) The Soviet Budget Macmillan, London

JURKOWICZ, P. (1982/83) 'Content and Characteristics of the Public Financing System' Eastern European Economics Vol.21, No.2, pp.3-49

KALETA, J. (1977) Budgetary Economics (Polish) State Economic Publishers, Warsaw

MUSGRAVE, R.A. (1969) Fiscal Systems Yale University Press, New Haven and London

OWSIAK, S. (1974) 'Parabudgets in the System of Financial Planning' Finanse, (Polish),

No. 5, May, pp.17-29
SWATLER, L. (1979) Finance in the Economic and Social Policy of the State (Polish) State Economic Publishers, Warsaw

Chapter 5

PRICING POLICY AND TAXATION

TURNOVER TAX AND RETAIL PRICES IN THE COMMAND MECHANISM

The turnover tax is a single-stage tax on sales of output of socialised enterprises to the retail market. Turnover tax has been, and continues to be, an important source of budgetary revenue in the socialist countries of the Soviet Union and Eastern Europe. This section discusses the 'traditional' form of turnover tax, used in the command mechanism. (Further discussion may be found in Adam, 1974 and Csikos-Nagy, 1975.)

In the command steering mechanism, turnover tax is an instrument of retail pricing policy, and is used to create a two-tier price structure. This two-tier price structure reflects two sets of principles of centralised pricing policy, one for retail prices, the other for producer prices, which produce a separate structure for each set of prices.

Producer prices are administered prices, set on the basis of cost-plus pricing rules devised by central planners. Retail prices are calculated by adding a further mark-up to producer price, to cover the profit of the socialised distribution network, and then adding the amount of turnover tax. The relationship between producer price and retail price may be shown by the equation:

$$RP = PP + RM + TT$$

where RP = retail price per unit of product
PP = producer price per unit
RM = profit margin of socialised distribution network

TT = the amount of turnover tax (price subsidies are treated here as a negative turnover tax)

Since RM can be assumed to be uniform (and normally is), turnover tax makes the difference between the structure of producer prices and the structure of retail prices.

The traditional turnover tax is a per unit tax, expressed as so many zlotys, roubles etc. per unit of product. In theory, central planners aim to set retail prices which clear consumer goods markets. The amount of turnover tax is determined by planned retail price, and is, in effect, a coded instruction about what retail price is to be charged. Retail price policy is also influenced by questions relating to the cost of living, and the distribution of real incomes, which are discussed on pp. 83-84 and 97-100.

The use of turnover tax to clear markets means that, in effect, the tax is used to distort the structure of consumer demand to bring demand in line with the structure of planned supply. In principle, turnover tax is calculated separately for each item, and a feature of traditional turnover tax in practice has been the great complexity of the system, with many thousands of separate tax rates, and highly selective taxation.

The traditional turnover tax system appears inefficient, from the viewpoint of conventional economics, since it distorts consumer choice. Conventional efficiency in allocation requires, inter alia, that supply adjust to demand, and that resources be allocated in line with consumer preferences. However, given the bounded rationality of planners, and the uncertainty and complexity of the real-world, it is certainly impossible to plan the output of consumer goods in line with consumer preferences; thus it may appear that consumer preferences must be forced into line with planned output. Inability to assess consumer preferences creates a form of information impactedness, which is then perpetuated by the sales tax system. If the structure of consumer goods output responds only to plan directives, the response function of the suppliers rules out any possibility that output can directly reflect consumer demand. Furthermore, because consumer demand is distorted by the turnover tax and the retail pricing system, consumer preferences are not reflected in markets, making it difficult for planners to discern preferences. Neglect of the consumer interest has probably been intensified by the priority which central planners have traditionally accorded to heavy industry, investment and economic growth.

In practice, turnover tax did not usually succeed in clearing markets. Generally, once the rate of turnover tax on a product was set, it was revised very infrequently, if at all, to reflect subsequent changes in market supply and demand. One possible reason is the high administrative costs which a regular review of many thousands of tax rates would have imposed. To the planners, the administrative costs of repricing would be far more visible than the efficiency costs of an inappropriate price structure. A further point is that central planners often exhibit a preference for price stability. In addition to the administrative costs of repricing, frequent price changes are alleged to create uncertainty and confusion, and may provoke resentment and social unrest which is not always expressed in a peaceful manner as Haddad (1977,p.51) has pointed out, and has been demonstrated by popular unrest in Poland in 1970, 1976 and 1980. From an economic viewpoint, if prices are changed to balance demand and supply, producers can influence price by restricting output, causing the classic inefficiencies of monopoly (Lipinski, 1977, p.165). Finally, changes in turnover tax may conflict with policies aimed at stabilising the cost of living, and may cause unplanned, and possibly unfair, changes in the distribution of real income.

It might be asked why the central authorities use turnover tax as an instrument of pricing policy at all. It would seem simpler to issue direct instructions on price. However, there are a number of possible reasons why an instruction in the form of a tax rate is preferred.

Firstly, it might be argued that the turnover tax is a single instrument which serves two policy purposes, namely, pricing policy and revenue-raising, and thereby saves on administrative costs. This is not such a convincing argument as it might appear. The socialist State has the entire profits of socialised enterprises at its disposal, and in the command system, enterprise residual profits are normally transferred to the State Budget. The division between turnover tax and enterprise after-tax profits is essentially arbitrary, since policy makers can manipulate rates of turnover tax to create whatever division they please (Bird, 1964, pp.204-205; Nove, 1977, p.232). In the absence of turnover tax, the established retail price would presumably be the same, and the State's budgetary revenue would not be diminished. It is hard to see that combining two functions in the turnover tax actually saves on administrative costs.

Secondly, turnover tax can be used to equalise profit margins on different lines of goods. This can be a consideration when plan targets are expressed in terms of profits, or where economic reforms are envisaged. If profit margins are unequal, artificial producer preferences may be created, leading producers to prefer high-margin products to low-margin ones. These producer preferences could contradict other preferences about the structure of output, be they planners' preferences or consumer preferences.

Thirdly, turnover tax forms part of the system of financial control. Planned turnover tax payments are established in the annual Budgetary Law, and actual payments constitute a flow of information to the State (as well as revenue). Variances between planned and actual revenue can be used to monitor implementation of financial plans. Moreover, turnover tax returns made by enterprises presumably contain reports of quantities, which can be used to monitor implementation of economic plans. Turnover tax returns are made regularly, and constitute a continuing and timely flow of information. In Poland, for example, turnover tax is paid quarterly, monthly, or every ten days, depending on the size of the enterprise, while in the Soviet Union, returns may be made as often as every three days.

Fourthly, Fedorowicz (1978, pp.336-337) has argued that the very structure of turnover tax rates conveys information about the extent and direction of distortion of consumer demand. This information gives some indication of consumer preferences, and conveys implied messages to central planners about the desirable direction of reallocation of resources. On this view, planners should expand output of goods bearing the highest rates of turnover tax, for which excess demand is, presumably, greatest. It is unlikely that the authorities have acted in the way Fedorowicz suggests, and, given the failure to review turnover tax rates regularly, in practice, the messages conveyed by turnover tax rates may have little informational content.

On the usual assumptions about the incidence of a sales tax, the economic incidence of the turnover tax rests on the purchaser of taxed goods, although the formal, or legal, incidence, rests on socialised enterprises. (Hutchings (1983, p.60) claims that this difference between economic and legal incidence enabled the Soviet Union to claim a reduction in taxes paid by the population when turnover tax was first introduced.) Turnover tax is normally levied only on domestically-produced and imported consumer goods, and not on industrial inputs, exports, or goods purchased by State bureaus. (However, Drabek claims that there are exceptions to this 'rule' - see 1979, esp. pp.19, 22, 25-27.) On the assumption that the tax is generally passed on to consumers, turnover tax is an important element in the balance of monetary income and expenditure of the population, and levels of turnover tax have implications for the overall stability and equilibrium of the consumer goods market generally, as well as for equilibrium in submarkets.

Rates of turnover tax are not generally published in socialist countries. It is generally believed that the structure of turnover tax is broadly redistributive, and that planners aim to charge low or negative turnover tax on basic necessities, while luxury goods usually bear high rates, especially if they are in excess demand. It is also believed that low or negative turnover tax is levied on 'merit' goods, so that, for example, books are subsidised in the interests of education and culture (Adam, 1974, pp.57-59). Drabek (1979) has attempted to estimate turnover tax rates from input-output data, and his estimated rates of turnover tax are not entirely consistent with these objectives. Although Drabek's results broadly confirm received wisdom as far as merit goods are concerned, he found (p.25) that some necessities, such as fuel, bore quite heavy turnover tax, while some non-necessities, such as consumer durables, were relatively lightly taxed. Heavy turnover tax on fuel may be designed to discourage non-industrial use, in order to give priority to industrial use.

In this section, several different functions of the traditional turnover tax have been outlined, not all of which are mutually consistent. Five main functions were detected: (1) as an instrument of pricing policy; (2) as an instrument for securing market equilibrium; (3) as a revenue-raiser for the State Budget; (4) as part of the system of financial planning, information and control; (5) to regulate interpersonal income distribution.

TURNOVER TAX AND REFORM OF THE STEERING MECHANISM

From the point of view of efficient resource allocation, the traditional turnover tax has certain disadvantages. Firstly, it drives a 'wedge' between producer prices and retail prices, so isolating producers from the markets for their products. Secondly, turnover tax is set to clear consumer goods markets by distorting consumer demand to make it conform to planned supply. One of the objectives of reform is to create greater consumer satisfaction by allowing output to respond to customer preferences, but the traditional turnover tax suppresses the relevant market signals. Reform of the steering mechanism thus requires reform of the turnover tax.

Reformers are generally agreed that (a) the rate of turnover tax should be an ad valorem rate, rather than a per unit rate, and (b) the number of rates in use should be reduced, so that overall, the structure of retail prices more closely resembles that of producer prices. (For example, see Fedorowicz and Orlowski 1970.) There is some controversy over whether the market clearing function of turnover tax should be retained, though this is a more important issue for the selectively decentralised mechanism, in which the central authorities retain greater control over prices than in market socialism. The arguments are connected with a debate over policies of 'price activism' versus policies of 'price neutrality' (Wanless, 1982, pp.95-101).

An active price policy, in this context, would use price signals to clear markets, inducing both quantity demanded and quantity supplied to adjust in the direction of equilibrium. Lange (1938) and Brus (1972) have both put forward mechanisms of this sort. Producers are instructed to maximise profits, and the central planning authority acts as a Walrasian auctioneer, raising prices for goods in excess demand, and cutting prices for goods in excess supply, until a set of market clearing prices are established. Turnover tax could be used to adjust market prices, in which case profits must be measured at 'market prices', rather than on a factor cost basis; that is, prices must be measured before deduction of turnover tax.

Proponents of price neutrality, on the other hand, argue that changes in relative profitability, associated with price activism, create artificial producer preferences about the structure of production. A more desirable solution, they allege, would be to strengthen the influence of consumer preferences on production. One suitable strategy would be to set producer prices on the basis of average production cost, impose uniform profit margins, and allow supply to respond to quantity signals, given by changes in customers' orders, or by changes in inventory. In principle, this solution requires either that profits be measured at 'factor cost' prices (i.e. after deduction of turnover tax) or that a single uniform rate of tax be imposed on all goods.

Price neutrality, it is claimed, would create a structure of prices which, being based on average cost, would approximate to the structure in long-term market equilibrium. Further, consumer welfare is more likely to be increased by expanding output at existing prices, than by raising prices and reducing real incomes to ration supply.

A price-neutral policy would economise on the bounded rationality of central planners. Prices would require adjustment only when levels of output had deviated significantly from the levels at which average costs were initially calculated. Lange's solution requires, in principle, that prices be recalculated every time supply or demand curves shift, a daunting task when thousands and thousands of different prices are involved. Apart from the high administration costs of such procedures, there are the adverse economic and social costs of frequent price changes. Moreover, suppliers could manipulate centrally determined price by withholding supplies from the market, causing the classic inefficiencies of monopoly.

Doubts may also be cast on the effectiveness of price changes in clearing markets. Leads and lags may prevent convergence on equilibrium, as illustrated by the well-known, 'cobweb theorem' or 'hog cycle' found in introductory economics textbooks. Fluctuations in supply and/or demand may be transitory or seasonal. So long as the product is not highly perishable, price adjustments may be unnecessary. Thus there may be a case for charging higher prices for tomatoes at the beginning and end of their season, but there is much less of a case for raising the price of bathing costumes in summer because of higher demand at that time.

A further point concerns the market for producer goods. The demand for producer goods is a derived demand, and so adjusting price is not necessarily a useful or suitable way of clearing the market, since adjustment to producer good prices would disturb the market for the final product.

A neutral price policy does not require turnover tax to clear individual markets, as markets are cleared by quantity adjustments. However, turnover tax could be used to establish equilibrium in the consumer goods sector as a whole. A single uniform ad valorem tax rate could be calculated to set the price-level of consumer goods at a level which would balance the money income and expenditure of the population. This single-rate turnover tax would be used for stabilisation purposes, being raised to 'mop up' any excess purchasing power which might otherwise cause inflationary pressure. In this respect, turnover tax would be a more appropriate instrument for changing prices than would the profit mark-up. Higher profit margins for firms, in the reformed mechanism, could lead to a price-wage inflationary spiral, because of the link between profits and wages.

One problem with the single rate solution is that there are, in practice, barriers to effective quantity adjustments. So long as strategic investment decisions remain entirely (or even largely) in the hands of central planners, the discretion of corporate managers to substitute among goods in production is limited to those goods which can be produced on the same set of technical equipment. Wanless, 1982, pp.121-123, outlines a solution to this problem, following Lipinski, 1977, pp.230-231. Turnover tax is levied at uniform rates within groups of products which can be produced with the same set of technical equipment but rates differ among product groups. The aim is to clear both the whole consumer goods sector, and very broadly defined markets for sets of related products. Another solution would be organisational rather than fiscal, namely allowing managers to diversify output at their own initiative. Hungary has recently given State corporations power to establish new subsidiaries, a solution which allows for greater flexibility in response to market forces.

In the market socialist mechanism, prices are market determined, and markets are cleared by price signals. Turnover tax is not required to set relative prices or clear individual markets. Reform of the turnover tax to promote uniform sales taxation remains important from the viewpoint of economic efficiency, since differences in rates of sales tax distort relative prices, and are a source of inefficiency. The economic theory of public finance generally predicts that a uniform sales tax results in a lower loss of efficiency than a multi-rate sales tax (e.g. Brown and Jackson, 1982, pp.240-247; 446-447).

Turnover tax could still perform a stabilisation function in a market socialist economy by regulating consumer purchasing power. Lange's solution would be achieved, but without the administrative costs. Some doubt may be cast on the efficiency of this solution, however, because of the monopoly power of large State corporations. (Incidentally, in the two economies which have avowedly adopted a form of market socialism, Yugoslavia and Hungary, some prices continue to be set by the central authorities, and many others are administered prices, set in accordance with centrally promulgated rules of cost-plus pricing). Overall, the role of turnover tax in price-setting and market-clearing becomes less important in reformed steering mechanisms, though the potential for a general stabilisation function *vis-a-vis* the consumer goods market remains. In practice, reform of consumer good prices has proceeded only slowly in the course of any attempt at reform. Per unit rates can be translated into ad valorem rates quite easily, and this in itself leads to a reduction in the number of rates of tax. For example, per unit rates of 5, 10, 15 zlotys on producer prices of 50, 100, and 150 zlotys are all equivalent to an ad valorem rate of 10%. Further reductions in the number of rates require changes in the relative prices of consumer goods, with possible price increases for some goods. This has generally led to gradual step-by-step reform of consumer goods prices, or even none at all.

Even where the overall aim of price policy is broadly neutral, elements of price activism could be introduced for special purposes. Around 1973-74, the Polish authorities used a form of price activism to try and improve the quality of goods produced, and to encourage product innovation. Goods designated as 'high quality' bore a reduced rate of turnover tax, so increasing the share of profit left at the disposal of the enterprise, and improving the synthetic indicator of performance. To encourage product innovation, producers were allowed to charge what the market would bear for new goods, which resulted in high profits. However, after two or three years, the goods ceased to be new (as far as the tax system was concerned). If the actual price charged exceeded a hypothetical price based on a standard cost-plus formula, the difference was creamed off as a 'supplementary turnover tax'. This was designed to encourage continued product innovation.

SUBSIDY POLICY AND REFORM

So far in this chapter, subsidies have been treated as negative turnover taxation. It is appropriate, however, to deal more explicitly with budgetary subsidies to current operations of socialised enterprise. (Budgetary subsidy of corporate investment is mentioned on pp. 107-8, while subsidised goods and services provided through State bureaus are dealt with in Chapter 1, and Chapter 4, pp.69-70.)

Operating subsidies can be divided into three types:-

(1) subsidies to cover operating losses of financially autonomous units.
(2) subsidies to hold down prices of selected goods and services.
(3) subsidies connected with guaranteed prices and price equalisation accounts.

Subsidies to cover operating losses are intended to be temporary, pending the return of the organisation to profitability, or its liquidation (usually by merger or reorganisation). Budgetary subsidies are made only as a last resort, as State corporations are intended to cover losses of constituent enterprises, by cross-subsidy from profitable ones. These kinds of budgetary subsidies may be termed 'subjective' subsidies (following Polish terminology), reflecting the fact that they are paid to an economic 'subject' (enterprise or corporation).

In contrast, subsidies to hold down prices of selected goods and services may be called 'objective' subsidies. They are normally paid per unit of output, so that customer price is below the price which would be established by the normal cost-plus pricing rules. Objective subsidies may be paid for industrial inputs, in order to keep down production costs. Subsidies of consumer goods may have redistributive aims, as when necessities such as food or children's shoes are subsidised; or subsidies may be paid to encourage meritorious consumption (e.g. of books). Objective subsidies prevent financially autonomous units from making losses as a result of producing the lines of products whose price is to be held down, and reduce disincentives to their production. In the context of economic reforms, objective subsidies of consumer goods pose a difficult problem of trading off equity against efficiency. Subsidies distort consumer preferences, but value judgements about income distribution or the merits of certain types of consumption may lead to a preference for continuing to subsidise. Objective subsidies of industrial inputs are difficult to justify on equity grounds, and seem undesirable on efficiency grounds, since underpricing can lead to an overlavish use of the subsidised product, which is wasteful and inefficient.

The third type of subsidy involves the use of the State Budget as a nationwide price equalisation account. This has been and continues to be a common feature of socialist countries, especially where the steering mechanism is of the command type.

A policy of price equalisation aims to guarantee or stabilise prices paid for, or received from the sale of, certain goods. The mechanics are simple. A standard, cost-plus price is established for the goods in question. Any supplier who sells at above the official price pays the difference as a tax to the State Budget, while a sale at a price below the official one attracts a compensatory subsidy. If purchases are made at advantageous prices, below the official ones, the difference is paid as a tax; but purchases at unfavourable prices, above official price, attract a compensating subsidy.

Price equalisation accounts have been extensively used in foreign trade in socialist countries, to insulate the domestic economy from the effects of fluctuations in world prices. However, price equalisation accounts are also found in domestic trade. Price equalisation accounts may be internal accounts within State corporations, which transfer funds from enterprises with below-average costs to those with above average costs. However, price equalising payments can also flow to and from the State Budget. In Poland, it appears that these types of payments have been used to hold down the prices of many consumer goods, including foodstuffs, in an attempt to control inflation (Wanless, 1982, pp.141-149).

These forms of price equalisation accounts

are found in socialist economies which broadly conform to the command stereotype, but their appropriateness is questionable once reform of the steering mechanism is envisaged, at least from the standpoint of allocative efficiency. Guaranteed prices reduce the incentive to search for the best markets, for cost-reducing innovations, and for more efficient techniques of production. Producers are isolated from market forces and from price signals. Abolition of price equalisation would improve the flow of market information to producers, which should improve economic efficiency. In pursuit of economic efficiency, Hungary abolished external price equalisation in the course of the 1968 reforms, but the subsequent policy of using world prices for all traded goods has not been followed consistently as world inflation has intensified. (Moreover, State corporations continue to operate internal price equalisation accounts.) Poland, in similar efficiency-minded reforms in 1973, also abolished external price equalisation accounts, only to introduce them again in 1975, as a response to rising world inflation. The policy trade-off here seems to be between micro-economic efficiency in production, and macroeconomic stabilisation.

PRODUCER PRICES AND TAXATION

In reforms of the steering mechanism, reforms of producer prices have been accorded as much, often more, attention than reform of retail prices. Producer prices are viewed as a direct influence on producer decisions, and discussion of the appropriate basis for price-setting abound. (A good summary is to be found in Abouchar, 1977). Policy-makers generally seem reluctant to leave the determination of prices entirely to market forces. Even in economies like Hungary, which have gone reasonably far down the road to market socialism, reform of producer prices has usually taken the form of issuing new rules of administered cost-plus pricing. Some of the costs of administering the price system were shifted from the central planners at the State Price Commission onto enterprise managers, who were given delegated authority to administer their own prices, in line with centrally devised rules. (See, for example, Hare, 1976; Hare and Wanless, 1981). Some reforms envisaged a certain amount of 'free pricing' which allowed freedom from administered pricing rules for some goods, and some special rules were devised for market novelties, principally by allowing higher profit margins to encourage product innovation.

In addition to the rules of cost-plus pricing, the centre can influence producer prices by means of taxes on factors of production, which influence the costs of production. Two such taxes commonly introduced in reforms of the steering mechanism are the tax on wages and the capital charge (see pp.37-38). These taxes are discussed in detail in Chapters 6 and 7, and will only be introduced here.

The taxes on factors of production perform a shadow pricing function for capital and labour. They influence the prices of factors faced by producers, the price received by producers and, ultimately, they are determinants of the structure of retail prices, since taxes on factors can be expected to be shifted forward in administered prices. (In market socialism, forward shifting of taxes might be less than 100%, and the effect on prices depends on relative elasticities of supply and demand).

One 'model' of administered pricing which embodies the possibility of forward shifting is the well-known 'two-channel' pricing system, often incorporated into reformed steering mechanisms. This involves two mark-ups on labour costs and capital cost, which have their counterpart in the wages tax and capital charge. Where two-channel pricing was proposed in Poland (in 1973) and Hungary (in 1968) the mark-ups were to be calculated in a way similar to the way the taxes were levied, that is related to labour costs and to the value of capital stock. (Hare and Wanless, 1981, pp.499-500).

The two-channel pricing system can be summarised by the equation:

$$PP = AC + a.K. + b.L$$

where PP = producer price
AC = average unit cost for the branch or industry
K = average unit capital cost

(usually calculated as fixed and working capital divided by output).
L = average unit labour cost

The mark-ups 'a' and 'b' are percentages, intended to represent 'required' or 'budget' profits. In theory, the mark-ups are uniform throughout the economy, and the policy-makers calculate the appropriate mark-up on the basis of economic aggregates planned for the economy as a whole. In practice, different rates may be charged for different branches. The mark-up 'a' can be calculated from planned investment, setting 'a' equal to I/K where I is planned investment, and K is the net value of the capital stock. (A slight variation would be to differentiate 'a' among branches to allow for differences in investment needs). The mark-up 'b' can be related to the 'indirect' or social costs of employing labour, which are borne collectively, and financed from the State Budget, such as employment, training, health care and other social expenditures.

Strictly speaking, two-channel pricing does not expressly include taxes on factors of production as determinants of producer price, and, on occasion, mark-ups 'a' and 'b' differed from the tax rates on wages and capital. This suggests a further way in which the State can manipulate the after-tax profit of State corporations. By raising 'a' and/or 'b' above the tax rates, (or cutting the tax rates) residual corporate profits can be increased; but if 'a' or 'b' are reduced (or tax rates increased) residual profits can be squeezed.

The relationship between mark-ups 'a' and 'b' and the rates of tax on wages and capital raises some interesting questions. In principle if 'a' or 'b' are set equal to the tax rates, then no after-tax profit is made at the level of output and utilisation of capital and labour for which 'a' and 'b' were calculated. This reinforces the incentives built into reform of the economic mechanism, to increase profit, and to economise on inputs of labour, fixed capital and working capital, which not only reduces actual costs below the standard costs built into administered prices, but also reduces tax liabilities.

In practice, however, where two channel pricing was actually used, the squeeze on residual profits was not made quite so strong as theory implies. For example, 'free' pricing was allowed for some goods, and in some cases e.g. Poland, 1973, the success indicator was measured gross of tax, rather than net.

Furthermore, mark-ups 'a' and 'b' would generally be set lower than the theoretical reasoning suggests. Since budgetary revenue is raised by other taxes, notably turnover tax, the entire burden of financing investment and social expenditures does not have to be recouped through taxes on producers' profit.

SUMMARY

This chapter has contrasted the role of taxation in price policy under the command steering mechanism and in reforms of the steering mechanism. In systems of administered pricing, taxes can be used by the central planners to manipulate price, with a variety of ends in mind. In 'neutral pricing' policy, taxes can be used to equalise profit margins, and to eliminate so-called 'producers' preferences'. In 'free market' pricing, when the central authorities relinquish administrative control over industrial prices, turnover tax should no longer be used to manipulate prices, except for the purposes of general stabilisation policy. Turnover tax is, however, not the only tax which can be used to influence price; producer prices can be influenced by taxes on factor inputs, as the last section of the chapter showed. The chapter also considered the use of price subsidies as equivalent to a negative turnover tax. It was argued that use of indirect tax for such purposes was undesirable on grounds of economic efficiency, but might be used for other reasons.

REFERENCES

ABOUCHAR, A. ed., (1977) The Socialist Price Mechanism Duke University Press, Durham, North Carolina

ADAM, J. (1974) Price and Taxation Policy in Czechoslovakia 1948-70 Duncker and

Homblot, Berlin
BIRD, R. (1964) 'The Possibility of Fiscal Harmonisation in the Communist Bloc' Public Finance Vol.19, pp.201-224
BROWN, C.V. and JACKSON, P.M. 1982 Public Sector Economics 2nd ed., Martin Robertson, Oxford
BRUS, W. (1973) The Market in a Socialist Economy Routledge and Kegan Paul, London and Boston
CSIKOS-NAGY, B. (1975) Socialist Price Theory and Price Policy Akademia Kiado, Budapest
DRABEK, Z., (1979) 'Estimation and Analysis of Turnover Tax in Centrally Planned Economies with Special Reference to Czechoslovakia' Public Finance Vol.34, pp.196-224
FEDOROWICZ, Z. (1978) The Economic-Financial Mechanism for Steering Economic Units (Polish) State Economic Publishers, Warsaw
FEDOROWICZ, Z. and ORLOWSKI, M. (1970) 'Recent Changes and Proposals for Change in the Administration of the Turnover Tax in Some Socialist Countries' Public Finance Vol.25, pp.307-318
HADDAD, L. (1977) 'Inflation Under Socialism' Australian Economic Papers Vol.16, No.28, pp.44-52
HARE, P.G. and WANLESS, P.T. (1981) 'Polish and Hungarian Economic Reforms: A Comparison' Soviet Studies Vol.32, pp.491-517
HUTCHINGS, R. (1983) The Soviet Budget Macmillan, London
LANGE, O. (1976) 'On the Economic Theory of Socialism' in O. Lange and F.M. Taylor On the Economic Theory of Socialism reprinted Tata-McGraw-Hill, New Delhi
LIPINSKI, T. (1977) Studies in Price Theory and Policy (Polish), State Economic Publishers, Warsaw
NOVE, A. (1977) The Soviet Economic System Allen and Unwin, London
WANLESS, P.T. (1982) Economic Policy and Taxation in Poland in the 1970s Strathclyde University Ph.D. Thesis

Chapter 6

WAGE POLICY, INCOME DISTRIBUTION AND TAXATION

WAGE POLICY IN REFORMED STEERING MECHANISM

Reform of the steering mechanism involves reforms in wage policy, and reform of taxes paid by enterprises (see pp. 23-28). The policy parameters relating to wage policy are the parameter k(or g) which relates changes in the wage fund to changes in profit, and the tax on the wage fund, WT. These parameters are inputs into the reponse function of producers, forming coded instructions about decisions relating to labour and wages. It is instructive to recall that Williamson (1975, Ch.2 passion) points out that one of the efficiency gains of internal decision-making comes from the use of 'in-house' codes or jargon; here we have an example of organisational change producing changes in the in-house 'code' which conveys instructions from planners to producers.

The reformed steering mechanisms contrast with the command model. In the command model, the total wage-bill for the economy is planned, with regard to planned real consumption, which is a residual, reflecting what is left of planned national income after allowing for planned accumulation (investment in heavy industry is usually a priority). Each employing organisation is given a plan target for expenditure on basic wages. This target reflects the anticipated number of workers, and their basic rates of pay, which are laid down in centrally determined wage tables. (Further details of this approach can be found in Kirsch, 1972; McAuley, 1979, Ch.8; McAuley, 1980, Chs 1, 2; Mehta, 1977, Ch.2). These tables specify the rate for each job, along with additions paid to workers with special qualifications, seniority payments, etc. (Sometimes rates of pay differ among industries or geographical regions, even for the same job, to reflect shortages or surpluses of labour). Over and above basic wages, bonuses are paid for plan fulfilment.

Pay scales are not necessarily characterised by a marked degree of egalitarianism. Workers who do relatively unskilled work, have little or no formal training, and have low productivity, tend to be ill-paid, outstripped in the pay race by skilled workers, managers, and so on. However, the ranking of occupations is not necessarily the same as in capitalist economies. Experience of socialist countries run on command lines reveals that engineers are better paid than doctors, but the reverse is usually true under capitalism. (This ordering presumably reflects the priority given to heavy industry, especially in the Stalinist period.)

That pay scales lack any apparent egalitarian bias is quite consistent with Marxist-Leninist doctrine. Marx is often quoted as favouring payment of workers according to need ('From each according to his ability: to each according to his need', Marx, 1974, p.17). But this is a principle applying only in full communism. Economies which call themselves socialist would claim to be in transition to communism. In the transitional stage, payment is based on work done (Marx, 1974, pp.15-17; Lenin, 1949, pp.87-90).

This Marxist-Leninist doctrine appears consistent with the new wage policy introduced by economic reforms, in which work done is measured by the synthetic indicator, net profit. To remind readers, reforms related changes in the wage fund to net profit by means of one of two formulae:

$$WF_1 - WF_0 = k.NP_1$$

or $$\frac{WF_1 - WF_0}{WF_0} = g\frac{NP_1 - NP_0}{NP_0}$$

where WF is the wage fund
NP is the net profit
0,1 are time subscripts, indicating the last period and current period

respectively
k,g are policy parameters or wage norms
($0<k,g<1$)

This formula relates to the wage bill for an entire corporation; the incentive provided is thus a collective one, and does not define individual remuneration, and the incentive effects must accordingly be weakened. State corporations in socialist countries can and do employ thousands of workers, distributed among dozens of work places, and the incentive-effect upon individual work effort must be very remote.

The change in the wage-fund determines the maximum increase in total remuneration which could be paid without incurring sanctions for excessive payment of wages. The wage-fund is a book-keeping creation, which has both a legal and economic significance, in that it defines and restricts the corporation's right to pay wages. Thus, general pay increases for successful enterprises (in the form of bonuses and/or basic pay increases) must be financed by improvements in net profit. The presumption seems to be that improvement in profit reflects productivity increases, in terms of quantity or quality of work done.

The value of policy parameter k (or g) is obviously an important policy issue. The setting of k and g at a value between 0 and 1 obviously ensures that some part of a firm's profit is saved and devoted to net capital formation. (We assume that replacement investment is financed from depreciation - a convenient simplifying assumption.) Net profit is measured after deduction of taxes paid to the State Budget, which finances collective consumption and capital formation. Thus the values of k and g must be related to plans for the share of individual consumption in national income.

In theory, values of k and g should be so that the wage-bill for the economy as a whole is balanced against the available supply of consumption goods, and the desired savings of households. Wage norms thus becomes instruments of stabilisation policy.

At prevailing price levels, if k (or g) is set too high, there will be excess demand in the consumer goods market, while if k(g) is set too low, there will be excess supply. The wage norms thus become important in maintaining equilibrium in the consumer goods market.

In setting k(g), the central authorities must decide whether the wage parameter is to have the same value throughout the economy, or whether it is to be individually addressed to corporations, with the wage norm set lower for corporations which can be expected to find it easy to raise profits, and higher for corporations facing more problems. Individually addressing the parameter has the theoretical advantage that equal increases in the wage fund can be made to reflect equal 'effort' by corporations, by making k lower for corporations which will find it easy to raise profits, and higher for corporations facing greater difficulties. However, the degree of difficulty must generally be assessed from information about markets, productive capacity and so on, which must come from the corporations themselves. This creates opportunities for opportunistic behaviour by corporate managers, who have an incentive to overstate their difficulties, so getting a high value for k and making it easier to earn higher profits, wages and bonuses. This opportunistic behaviour is a disadvantage of using individually addressed parameters. (This kind of opportunism occurred in the Polish reforms of 1973-75; see Wanless, 1980, p.42).

A further problem is that the incentive system, while apparently satisfying the criteria of payment according to work done, means that wage rates in different corporations can diverge by considerably more than was envisaged when the original national pay scales were established. This raises the question of whether personal income taxation should be used to reduce these divergences e.g. through progressive tax rates. Both moral principles and political expediency may suggest that the gap between the successful (or lucky) and the unsuccessful (or unlucky) should not be allowed to become too great. However, progressive personal income taxation may weaken work incentives yet further. (Albania, Poland and Romania have generally ablished personal income taxation for employees in the socialised sector, so these countries have abandoned one instrument of distribution policy.) Another solution is to have periodic 'wage adjustments' on grounds of comparability, a solution which is less likely to weaken incentives, and overcomes problems of resentment and envy among workers.

WAGES TAX IN REFORMED STEERING MECHANISMS

The wages tax is one of the four taxes of reformed steering mechanisms, which are deducted in measuring the synthetic indicator of performance, net profit:

$$NP = (R-TC) - TT - CT - WT - PT$$

where NP is net profit
R is sales revenue
TC is total costs
TT is turnover tax (net of objective price subsidies)
CT is capital tax
WT is wages tax
PT is profits tax

The four taxes between them transfer funds to the State Budget. As part of the Budget's role in the division of national income, they supply funds for collective expenditure and Budget-financed capital accumulation. The turnover tax has already been discussed at some length. The only additional point to make here is that, in the formula, sales are measured on the basis of producer prices, rather than consumer prices. The advantages of this are, firstly, that enterprise profit is not artificially raised or lowered by changes in turnover tax, and, secondly, producer preferences are not created by differences in turnover tax on different lines of goods.

Capital taxes and profits tax are discussed in the next chapter, and this section will concentrate on the role of the wages tax.

In reformed mechanisms, wages tax is a general payroll tax, which can influence the relative price of labour. The base of the tax may be defined slightly differently to the wage fund in the previous section; being defined either as wages paid, or as the notional wage fund. A payroll tax creates a shadow price of labour in excess of the wage actually paid. (We assume downward rigidity of money wages, due to institutional constraints.) If the wage actually paid is W, and the payroll tax is levied at rate t_w, then the shadow price of labour SPL is $SPL = W(1 + t_w)$.

There are various possible reasons for this shadow pricing which, ceteris paribus, will tend to induce producers to economise on labour input, and adopt less labour-intensive techniques of production.

Firstly, it is argued that the social cost of labour is greater than the wage actually paid. The State provides collective consumption goods and social services for workers, such as health care, education and training, family allowances, etc. A tax on wages, it is argued, is necessary to cover these 'indirect' costs of labour. This is apparently an application of the 'benefit' principle of taxation, though a somewhat dubious one. Expenditure on collective consumption and social services does not necessarily vary systematically with the total wage bill in the economy, and it is not clear that a tax on the wage-bill is an appropriate way of financing them.

Secondly, a wages tax may be a response to labour shortage. Actual wages paid may represent distributional objectives rather than allocative decisions, and there may be ideological objections to raising wages actually paid. The level of wages may be regarded as something which should be related to the needs of families, or to notions of social justice. Moreover, if we consider the principle of payment according to work done, labour shortage does not increase the quantity or quality of work, and is not an obvious reason for paying increased wages.

Labour shortage may arise for a variety of reasons. One possible cause is 'taut planning' (the practice of setting unrealistically high plan targets in order to elicit large outputs). Another is the stage of development of the socialist economy, which may have exhausted the possibilities for transferring underemployed labour from the rural to the industrial sector. Demographic factors, such as a drop in the birth rate, are a further cause of labour shortage. Whatever the cause, raising the shadow price of labour can be a rational response to labour shortage.

Thirdly, shadow pricing of labour allows wages paid to differ from the marginal product of labour, without sacrificing economic efficiency. Simple Paretian welfare criteria require that the wage on which producers base allocative decisions be equal to the marginal product of labour. However, in order to promote economic growth, planners may wish to restrict consumption and raise the level of investment (or, in Marxist terms, to raise the share of accumulation in national income). Paying wages below the marginal product of labour is one way of achieving this.

Finally, a tax on wages may be a way of tackling problems of labour hoarding. Under the command mechanism, hoarding labour is rational for managers, since a pool of in-house underemployed labour allows some flexibility, and facilitates the achievement of plan targets. A tax on wages can be a way of promoting a shake-out of surplus labour. A similar argument underlay the Selective Employment Tax introduced in Britain in the 1960s, which had the added refinement of trying to transfer labour out of the service sector into manufacturing (which escaped SET and even, for a time, received a wage subsidy).

It should be noted that a payroll tax will only have the effects described above if it actually raises the shadow price of labour. In economic reforms, wages tax was introduced at a time when other new taxes were being introduced, or rates and rules of existing taxes were being changed. Sumner, in commenting on Britain's SET, has pointed out (1983 pp.16-17) that SET largely failed because contemporaneous changes in rules for capital allowances in respect of fixed investment resulted in a rise in the price of capital, which he claims largely offset the reallocative effects of SET. The introduction of packages of complex tax changes can have effects which really require a general equilibrium approach, a topic which takes us far outside the scope of this book, and beyond the scope of much established public finance theory.

There may be other restraints on the effectiveness of the shadow pricing function of the wages tax. If pricing arrangements allow the wage tax to be shifted forwards to consumers, then there is no incentive to economise on labour input, or hardly any, since wages tax will not reduce profits. In addition, there may be institutional restrictions on dismissing labour, so that any reduction in the size of the labour force must take place slowly, through a combination of natural wastage and reduced recruitment.

Payroll taxes are normally levied at proportionate rates, that is, as a percentage of the wages bill. However, there are other possibilities; the tax rate could be made progressive with regard to the size of the wage bill (as with the tax on wage increases in the Hungarian reforms of 1968) or the tax paid could be related to the numbers in employment. Both these variants would serve to intensify incentives to economise on labour input as the size of the work force grew, and the progressive tax would also serve as a brake on wage increases, which might serve purposes of economic stabilisation. However, these variants might have adverse effects at corporate level in terms of the desiderata of the reformed mechanisms (assuming no forward shifting). Growth of the work-force in some corporations may be required to adapt supply to shifts in customer demand, while progressive payroll taxes place a tax on wage increases and could well weaken the incentive system further.

INDIRECT TAXATION AND INCOME DISTRIBUTION

The system of turnover taxation and price subsidies determines the level and structure of retail prices (see Ch. 5) and thus provides the Central Planners with an instrument for regulating the level of real wages and the standard of living of the population. In principle, this instrument is also available to promote interpersonal equity, by regulating the interpersonal distribution of real incomes. For example, low taxation (or subsidised prices) of 'necessities' such as food, fuel, children's clothing etc. is seen as favouring the poor. If this is combined heavy taxation of 'luxuries' such as consumer durables, cameras, jewellery, etc., the indirect tax system appears to promote vertical equity. Taxing 'luxuries' consumed by the rich while subsidising basic 'necessities' which figure prominently in the family budgets of the poor, is often seen as a socially desirable strategem, by socialist and capitalist governments alike.

However, in many ways, it is surprising to find that socialist governments adopt this practice. It appears completely inappropriate to use impersonal taxation to promote interpersonal equity. After all, the rich consume 'necessities', often in larger quantities than the poor. They eat more and of a better quality; they are better able to afford to heat their houses, and use more electricity; the children of the rich have more clothes. Similar arguments apply to almost any 'necessity' one can think of. Housing - the rich have larger houses: medicine - the rich make more use of health care. Moreover, the poor often consume the heavily taxed 'luxuries', especially consumer durables. Regardless of the steering mechanism of the socialist economy under consideration, it would seem more appropriate to use other instruments of distribution policy (such as wage policy and social security policy) as a means of promoting interpersonal equity. Impersonal indirect taxation is a very inferior instrument for this purpose. Moreover, there may be a clash with other potential functions of turnover taxation.

As we have seen (Chapter 5), in the command mechanism of the socialist economy, the turnover tax is, in theory, used to clear markets. Tax rates are set highest for goods with the most marked degree of excess demand; but these are not necessarily 'luxuries'. (Although they might well be, if the Plan gives high priority to production of necessities, and low priority to luxury production. This seems quite a reasonable ordering of priorities.) Subsidised prices of necessities will normally create excess demand for these products, demand in excess of the socially optimal level. Hence, there are potential conflicts between using indirect taxes (and subsidies) to promote interpersonal equity and using them to clear markets.

A further point is that public finance theory teaches us that differential sales taxation is less efficient than uniform taxation, involving a greater distortion of consumer choices, and a greater loss of consumer welfare.

In the selectively decentralised and market socialist models, efficiency is a key policy objective, and uniform sales taxation is preferable. Subsidies to maintain artificially low prices for 'necessities' such as food also run counter to the requirements of efficiency, boosting demand to the point where the marginal social benefits of consumption are lower than marginal social cost. Once again, objectives concerned with interpersonal distribution would seem better served by relying on alternative policy instruments.

Socialist economies which have moved in the direction of the decentralised or market socialist system, such as Poland and Hungary, have usually introduced changes in the system of turnover taxation and price subsidies, or at least a declaration of intent to change. Price subsidies are phased out, or much reduced in scope, while turnover tax is simplified, and the number of rates reduced. The phasing out of price subsidies involves, of course, increases in the prices of previously subsidised goods - something which can provoke popular unrest and opposition. The Hungarian authorities appear to have handled these problems more tactfully than the Polish authorities. In Hungary, consumer price increases were compensated by wage increases, especially for the lower paid. In Poland, on the other hand, increases in consumer prices, especially foodstuffs, became a focus for popular discontent in 1970, 1976 and 1980; price increases were cancelled as a result. In 1982 retail price increases were very marked, but successfully implemented under martial law.

Nevertheless, in spite of some economic reforms, price subsidies for necessities are common throughout socialist economies. They cover not only basic consumer goods, such as food, but also basic industrial goods, for example, cement, iron ore, coal and oil. (Thus some producer prices are also subsidised.) Exactly which necessities are subsidised varies from time to time, and country to country. The reason for their continued existence is a matter of speculation. Subsidy has for long been a common feature, so common that it may be simply unquestioned, unchallenged and taken for granted. Subsidies may be maintained because they enable the prices of necessities to remain stable, and help promote overall price stability, bringing with it certain social and political advantages.

Whatever the perceived advantages of continuing price subsidies, there is a cost. Price subsidies distort consumer preferences, and impair the effectiveness of market forces. They promote inefficiency in consumption, and inefficiency in production. If producers base their decisions on the subsidised price, the artificially created producer preference against the subsidised good worsens the problem of excess demand. (There will usually be excess demand for subsidised goods; but in the case of merit goods and goods generating positive externalities, efficiency requires subsidies to raise demand to socially optimal levels.)

Overall, considerations of interpersonal equity do not justify the complex and extensive system of differentiated turnover tax and price subsidies which is or has been observed in socialist economies, such as those of the Soviet Union and Eastern Europe. Influence over personal incomes is a better weapon for promoting interpersonal equity. The efficiency costs of such a system also render it undesirable.

INCOME DISTRIBUTION, PERSONAL TAXATION AND SOCIAL SECURITY

In the economic theory of public finance, one of the presumed aims of the tax system is the promotion of equity (see Brown and Jackson, 1982, pp.62-67, and 216). 'Vertical equity' is a principle of fair or equitable taxation, based on differential taxation of those with differing ability to pay. At the same time, it is argued, the tax system should promote horizontal equity; that is, those of equal ability to pay should bear an equal tax burden.

In capitalist economies, personal income taxation is often viewed as an important instrument of income distribution policy. Vertical equity is promoted by progressive taxation of personal incomes, complemented by taxes on wealth to bring capital gains and the non-pecuniary advantages of wealth ownership within the tax net. The question of horizontal equity is related to the definition of the tax base, and the tax-paying unit (see for example, Kay and King, 1983, p.68-81, 211-215).

On the face of it, a socialist State has less need of personal income taxation to promote equitable distribution. Income from wages and salaries can be controlled through centralised wages policy and national pay scales. Property (unearned) income is much less common in socialist countries than in capitalist ones, since, in socialist countries the means of production are socially owned and there is no capital market. Thus opportunities for the accumulation and bequeathing of large amounts of wealth are limited. Overall, a socialist government seems to have rather less need of personal income taxation than a capitalist government. Indeed, one might argue that personal income taxation is inappropriate in a socialist society.

However, even with the socialist State's control over wages policy, its control over incomes is imperfect. Individuals may hold more than one job, and there may be more than one wage earner per household. Some forms of property income do survive e.g. rent from letting rooms, interest on savings, or property income from abroad (as in the case of retirement pensions of Polish Americans who have chosen to spend their retirement in their native land.) Incomes earned in the private sector are to some extent outside State control, especially as far as the earnings of the self-employed are concerned. In the course of economic reforms, central control over wages is somewhat weakened, as wages paid are linked to the synthetic indicator; in this case, the centralised wage table sets minimum, rather than actual, rates.

Thus the socialist State may wish to complement wage policy with tax policy, in pursuit of an equitable distribution of income. Further, it might be argued that wage policy should concern itself with efficiency rather than equity issues. The Marxist principle of payment according to work done would seem to point to wages based on efficiency, rather than equitable considerations. This again suggests that tax policy could be used to promote interpersonal equity, if policy-makers consider this a desirable end in itself.

The importance of taxation in interpersonal distribution varies. Chapter 3 showed that the importance of personal taxation in budgetary revenues differs from country to country. Poland and Romania have largely abolished personal income taxation, and so too has Albania. These countries have apparently decided to forego the use of taxation as an instrument of redistributive justice. But Poland, for example, has abolished personal income tax only for an individual's primary employment in the socialised sector - an arrangement which may be connected with administrative economies. In Poland, income from second, third, etc. jobs remains liable to tax, as are incomes earned in the private sector, and income from property. In addition, Poland levies a 'surtax' on the total income of high income recipients, regardless of whether their income is or is not liable to income tax. The Polish case illustrates the use of taxation to enhance the State's control over interpersonal distribution. (Poland also taxes wealth, by means of inheritance taxes, and stamp duties on property transfers). However, given the types of income which remain liable to income tax in Poland, tax evasion may be a severe problem.

The abolition of income tax in socialist countries alters the structure of taxation, reducing personal taxation and increasing business taxation, principally taxes on State corporations. This was made quite explicit in the Polish case, where a separate and distinct payroll tax was levied on State corporations, expressly to compensate for revenue lost through the phasing out of personal income taxation for most State employees between 1972 and 1976. Initially this tax was levied at individually addressed rates, based on the income tax revenue collected from each corporation before abolition. Later (1977), rules were standardised, and in 1982, this tax was belatedly merged with a further wages tax introduced as a result of economic reforms in 1974.

Abolition of personal income tax has certain advantages. Firstly, it enables the authorities to claim a certain propaganda victory, claiming that workers in a socialist State are not 'exploited' by being forced to pay income tax, in the way that workers in a capitalist economy are. (However on any reasonable assumption about tax incidence increased business taxes will almost certainly be passed on to customers especially where business taxes are treated as costs in calculating cost-plus prices).

Secondly, it may be argued that abolition promotes economic efficiency and work effort, since the marginal rate of tax becomes zero.

Thirdly, there are economies in tax administration to be made, since, by shifting from personal to business taxation, the number of tax-payers is much reduced, with consequent savings in cost of assessment, collection costs, communication costs, etc. Thus there is case for abolition on grounds of administrative, as well as economic efficiency. These efficiency gains are compromised, however, when, as in the Polish case, some taxation of income from work is retained, presumably on grounds of vertical equity.

A second instrument of equitable distribution policy is the system of social security (which can be treated as negative taxation). Like personal income tax, this is an instrument which seems (qualitatively) less important in a socialist state than in a capitalist one, where social security is often seen as an instrument of vertical equity, as a remedy for poverty, and includes government subsidies in cash or in kind even to those in work (for example, the US 'food stamps' programme, and Britain's Family Income Supplement). In socialist countries centralised wage policy can solve the problem of low pay, though at some efficiency cost, if the socially desirable minimum wage exceeds the marginal product of labour. This kind of inefficiency would also presumably violate the Marxist principle of payment according to work done.

In socialist countries, social security still has a vertically equitable anti-poverty stance, in that one of its functions is to provide incomes for those who cannot work, either because of temporary incapacity (e.g. due to illness or pregnancy) or for more permanent reason (chronic illness, physical disability, or old age). However the concept of providing for the unemployed, or the low paid does not seem to enter into social security policy;

apparently, the solution to these problems is seen to lie in central planning of employment and wages, despite potential conflicts between equity and efficiency.

The social security system also promotes horizontal equity, principally through a system of child allowances paid in respect of dependent children. In this way, family income can be related to family needs and family size, while, in principle, wage income can be related to work performed. Taken to its logical conclusion, social security policy could be used to reconcile efficiency and equity conflicts in distribution policy. In contrast, a policy of 'equitable' wages violates efficiency, and may not adequately reward work effort. Personal income taxation is also at a disadvantage, compared to social security policy, since income taxation imposes distorting marginal tax rates; systems of social security can reduce these distortions (provided benefits are not means-tested, and the 'poverty trap' can be avoided). It appears that reform of the steering mechanism to secure allocative efficiency could be facilitated by reforms of the social security system to secure distributive justice, though reform attempts do not appear to have incorporated such ideas.

As in capitalist countries, social security is funded, in whole or in part, by specially earmarked social security contributions. However, in socialist countries, social security contributions are often paid by employers, usually as a straightforward payroll tax, though GDR uses both employer and employee contributions. Like the wages tax in reformed mechanisms, social security contributions raise the shadow price of labour, though there is perhaps a stronger case for claiming that this represents a payment to cover 'indirect' costs of labour, in this case, the costs of social security system. Public finance theory (e.g. Musgrave 1959, p.311) predicts that, in market systems, selective taxes on a factor will normally be passed forward to customers, while in systems of administered pricing, social security contributions are normally treated as an element of labour costs and passed on to consumers in cost-plus prices. No matter which steering mechanism of the socialist economy is under consideration, it appears that consumers ultimately pay for the social security system. Since consumers are presumably also workers, it might be argued that this is justifiable under the principle of taxation according to benefit, a principle of equitable taxation which is an alternative to the ability-to-pay principle.

SUMMARY

This chapter has outlined the role of wage taxation and wages policy in 'command' and 'reformed' mechanisms. Wages tax is found to occur in a variety of forms - as wage-fund tax, social security contributions, and as personal income tax. In its different forms, a tax on wages can be used for efficiency purposes by changing the 'shadow price' of labour, or for equity purposes, by influencing interpersonal distribution.

REFERENCES

BROWN, C.V. and JACKSON, P.M. (1982) Public Sector Economics 2nd ed. Martin Robertson, Oxford

KAY, J.A. and KING, M.A. (1983) The British Tax System 3rd. ed., Oxford University Press

KIRSCH, L.J. (1982), Soviet Wages: Changes in Structure and Administration since 1956 MIT Press, Cambridge, Mass. and London

LENIN, V.I. (1949) The State and Revolution Progress Publishers, Moscow

MARX, K. (1974) Critique of the Gotha Programme Foreign Languages Press, Peking

MCAULEY, A. (1979) Economic Welfare in the Soviet Union Allen and Unwin, London

MCAULEY, A. (1980) Women's Work and Wages in the Soviet Union Allen and Unwin, London

MEHTA, V. (1977) Soviet Economic Policy: Income Differences in the USSR Radiant Publishers, New Delhi

MUSGRAVE, R.A. (1959) The Theory of Public Finance McGraw-Hill Kogakusha International Student Edition, Tokyo

SUMNER, M.T. (1983) 'The Incentive Effects

of Taxation' in R Millward et al Public Sector Economics Longman, London and New York

WANLESS, P.T. (1980) 'Economic Reform in Poland 1973-1979' Soviet Studies Vol.32, No.1, pp.28-57

WILLIAMSON, O.E. (1975) Markets and Hierarchies: Analysis and Anti-Trust Implications Free Press, New York

Chapter 7

TAXES ON CAPITAL AND PROFITS

CAPITAL CHARGES

Taxes on capital employed, usually known as capital charges, have been levied on socialised enterprises in the socialist economies of the Soviet Union and Eastern Europe since around the 1960s. Introduced as part of a wave of early and largely abortive reform attempts, capital charges have survived, sometimes, even when other aspects of reform have failed. Capital charges were introduced to improve the mechanism of investment planning and finance, and to lead to a more efficient allocation of investment.

Efficiency requires that investment be allocated to projects whose rate of return exceeds the opportunity cost of capital. In the theory of a market economy, the opportunity cost of capital is indicated by the market rate of interest, and capital markets function to allocate (money) capital to the most productive uses. In a socialist economy, there is no market interest rate to indicate the opportunity cost of capital, and investment allocations are largely centrally planned (though managers may have some delegated powers of investment, usually for small-scale projects). In socialist economies run along command lines, investment planning prior to the introduction of capital charges lacked some of the elements of a rational basis. Plan targets for investment were generally specified in expenditure terms, there was little or no account taken of the profitability of investment, and, indeed, in the absence of an opportunity cost of capital, no basis for judging whether projects were profitable or not. Managers at corporate or enterprise level had no interest in the cost of investment, since investment finance was supplied by means of an interest free grant from the State Budget. Moreover, the profitability of investment was a matter of indifference to them, since enterprise gross profits were transferred, in their entirety, to the State Budget, and their performance was not judged by profits, but by specialised indicators such as output. Managers did have an interest, however, in pressing planners to maximise their target investment expenditures, since a lavish stock of assets made it easier to fulfil, and overfulfil, plan targets for output. Thus there was a built-in pressure leading to waste and inefficiency in investment, and a corresponding tendency to underutilisation of the existing capital stock.

Reforms of investment have generally involved changes in planning and changes in financing. In planning, indicators of the profitability of investment were introduced, generally based on discounted cash flow investment appraisal. Budgetary financing was discontinued, or, at least, its scope was reduced, in favour of so-called 'self-financing', under which centrally planned investment at corporate or enterprise level was financed either by bank loans, repayable with interest, or out of retained profits (which were paid into a special development fund' for each organisation.) The administered interest rate on bank loans provided a target rate of return on investment.

A corresponding capital charge, or shadow price of capital was introduced on investments financed by profit retentions, so that all investment funds bore a target rate of return or opportunity cost of capital. Thus the profitability of investment could be used as a criterion in investment planning. Further, when combined with the use of synthetic indicators of performance, the financial costs of investment go some way towards discouraging excessive investment, though this depends, in part, on how readily available bank loans are.

Investments were made self-liquidating. In the case of investments financed by bank loans, the original capital outlay was repaid out of depreciation provisions, which were used to finance instalment repayments of the loan. For profit-financed investments, depreciation provisions were used to 'repay' the organisation's development fund, so that depreciation and profit retentions provided a continuing pool of investment finance.

Where they are used, capital charges are normally levied on both fixed capital (net of any outstanding long-term bank loans) and on net working capital (that is, current assets minus short-term bank credits). However, Poland taxed fixed capital only and abolished even that charge in 1982 and replaced it by a real estate tax. Hungary abolished its capital charges in 1980. The tax base is normally the book value of assets, on an historical cost basis. In the case of fixed assets, this raises the choice between the original undepreciated cost of the asset, or the net book value (i.e. written-down value). The choice of tax base can, in principle, have implications for the quality of investment decisions.

Two disadvantages have been attributed to the use of written-down value (e.g. by Bajgusz, 1977). Firstly, it makes the tax base depend on the accounting conventions governing depreciation. Secondly, since the tax burden declines as assets grow older, new investment imposes an additional financial burden, and so, it is argued, capital charges discourage new investment and damage innovation and modernisation.

The first criticism is probably unimportant, since depreciation rules can be established by the central authorities and can be framed to suit the ends of economic policy (Fedorowicz, 1978, ch.7). The authorities in Britain also manipulate depreciation rules for policy purposes, through the system of capital allowances allowed against corporation tax.

The second point is accepted by those who favour the use of written-down value (e.g. Fedorowicz, 1978, p.273; Wakulska, 1975, p.45) but they see this feature as an advantage, rather than a disadvantage. If 'old' fixed assets bear lower tax than 'new' fixed assets, then, it may be argued, new assets will be purchased only if they are more productive than old ones, by a margin sufficient to compensate for the higher capital charge. This acts as a further counter to tendencies to overinvestment, endemic in the 'command' mechanism. Such arguments, may, however, be fallacious. The use of written-down value may equalise the costs of 'old' and 'new' assets, rather than create a differential, since, although the capital charge declines as assets age, maintenance costs increase. Thus the lower cost of 'old' fixed assets may be illusory.

The use of written-down value may be justified on the grounds of equal treatment of loan-financed and profit-financed investments. Once a loan-financed assets is fully depreciated, the original loan has been paid off by accumulated depreciation provisions, and no further interest is payable. Equally, it may be argued that when a profit-financed investment is fully depreciated, the accumulated depreciation provisions have repaid the original cost, so no further capital charge should be levied.

The choice of tax rate is also an issue. This issue raises problems similar to problems encountered in selecting the appropriate discount rate in cost-benefit analysis, which is also an exercise in shadow pricing for cost of capital. Cost-benefit analysis offers us the guideline that the discount rate (or capital charge) should reflect the marginal social rate of time preference, in order to fulfil Paretian criteria for optimal intertemporal resource allocation (Feldstein, 1964). In policy-making in Eastern Europe, a rather different approach has been used, derived from the Marxist model of expanded reproduction (economic growth). In this approach, profits are the source of economic growth, and the target rate of return is set equal to the desired rate of growth of the capital stock. Profits are thus assumed to finance the growth of the capital stock, and policy-makers can calculate the appropriate capital charge, CT, from the formula:

$$CT = \frac{I}{K'}$$

where I is planned net investment in fixed and working capital
K' is the net value of the capital stock

This approach has operational advantages, since CT can be calculated from measurable quantities, and is not based on an unmeasurable, subjective concept like the marginal social rate of time preferences.

However, there are some conceptual difficulties. Consider the case where the authorities wish to increase the level of net investment. Assuming that enterprises are profit maximising, we would expect the authorities to reduce the target rate of return on investment, and managers would accordingly increase invesment. However, the Marxist approach outlined above suggests that an increase in planned investment leads to an increase in the target rate of return, which would seem discouraging to investment.

This apparent paradox can be resolved to some extent. The view that a fall in target return is needed to bring about an increase in investment is derived from neo-classical economics, in which managers/entrepreneurs have discretion over investment spending. The paradox vanishes if we assume that investment planning and investment policy represent strategic decisions, taken entirely at central planning level. If that were the case, managers would have no discretionary powers of investment, and the possibility of the capital charge giving the 'wrong' price signal to managers does not arise. Raising the capital charge has the effect (at the macro-economic level) of reducing the share of wages in national income, and makes it possible for the central planners to raise investment at the expense of consumption. Standard growth theory predicts that this will raise the rate of economic growth. The paradox thus vanishes.

However, reforms of the steering mechanism often allow managers some discretion over unplanned investment spending on a small scale. In principle, the paradox can arise. However the paradox is unlikely to be important in those cases where managerial discretion is quite circumscribed. In most reforms, discretion was only offered to rather small-scale investments of a type which have no overall strategic importance. Further limits may be imposed on managerial discretion by special taxes. (The Polish reforms of 1973 incorporated such a tax. Up to a threshold level, unplanned investment spending was tax-free, but further spending was taxed at 80-90%.) Bank supervision of spending of investment funds is a further restraint on managerial discretion. However, Hungary's 'market socialist' type of reforms allowed considerable managerial discretion over investment, so the paradox may not be altogether insignificant.

Whether any decentralisation of investment is desirable is debatable. Remarks by Lange (Lange and Taylor, 1976, pp.105-106) suggest that any such decentralisation is undesirable, because of the potentially destabilising effect of a market-determined business cycle. Experience suggests, however, that centrally-planned economies can generate cyclical movements of their own - see Bajt, 1971 and Anderson,1983. Nevertheless, limited decentralisation relieves the central administration of the costs of small-scale investment decisions, and confers power and prestige upon managers, which can improve morale and managerial calibre.

A further point is that, without a capital market, the socialist economy apparently lacks a decentralised mechanism for intertemporal resource allocation, which must inevitably involve changes in economic structure, and shifting control over financial and physical resources from one 'branch' to another. In a planning system, this is almost invariably a Head Office function, and in a socialist economy, it would seem that intertemporal allocation should remain a central planning function. Interestingly, however, Hungary seems to be setting a trend towards decentralisation of such strategic decisions. Hare, 1983, pp.325-326, reports that Hungarian State corporations have been granted power to establish new subsidiaries. In the area of investment finance, a market in bonds issued by State corporations has been established (The Banker, May 1983, p.87), though with the restriction (initially, at any rate) that bonds can only be sold to other State corporations. It remains to be seen how permanent such changes are, and whether other socialist countries will follow Hungary's example.

Capital charges were introduced in most Comecon countries in the 1950s and 1960s, as part of a wave of attempts at economic reform. In some cases, capital charges survived long after reforms had failed and recentralisation had occurred. For example, the GDR and USSR both still use capital charges, though the USSR is generally regarded as a highly centralised command economy, and the GDR's capital charges formed part of its 'New Economic System' which, introduced in the late 1960s, was rapidly followed by a return to recentralisation (see Leptin and Meltzer, 1978, passim). Poland introduced capital charges in the late 1950s, and incorporated them into the economic reforms of 1973-75. Capital charges contined to be levied until 1982, when they were abolished and replaced by a real estate tax; thus capital charges survived for many years of decentralisation and recentralisation in the 1960s and 1970s. Interestingly, Hungary, with its successful reforms, nevertheless abolished capital charges in 1980. Capital charges are sometimes criticised on the grounds that, when they are treated as an element of cost, they increase prices in capital-intensive industries relative to prices in labour intensive industries (Leptin and Meltzer, pp.91-92). This, however, appears to be a desirable effect, if capital costs are to be adequately reflected in prices.

PROFITS TAX

The term 'profits tax', used here, requires a little clarification. Firstly, the term profits tax, or deductions from enterprise profits, is used in some socialist countries to cover payments which are straight transfers of profit, depreciation and similar items, and which are not taxes as we defined them on pp. 1-4. (See for example, Birman, 1981, pp.26-32). Secondly, unlike, say, turnover tax and capital charges, the kind of profits tax envisaged here is not particularly standardised among economic systems, not even among attempted or successful reform mechanisms. We use here a theoretical construct, a tax on net profits, to enable us to draw some conclusions about a shift from a command mechanism, in which the State Budget is normally the residual beneficiary of profit, to a reformed mechanism, in which the corporation or enterprise is the residual beneficiary, and the State's share is defined by the rules of taxation. Without this simplifying device, the discussion would likely be highly involved in discussing the complexities of different forms of profits taxation. (For example, some reforms, such as Poland, 1973, and Hungary, 1968, did not tax profits per se, but rather taxed the 'funds' formed out of profits - see Hare and Wanless, 1981, especially, pp.507-508. However, the niceties of such distinctions are probably not essential for the points made here.)

In what follows, I shall assume that State corporations pay profits tax on their net profits. After-tax profits remain at the disposal of State corporations and enterprises, and are used to finance bonuses, pay increases and investment, along the lines indicated in pp. 23-28. This contrasts with the 'command' mechanism, in which 'after-tax profits' were simply transferred wholesale to the State Budget, and the distinction between taxes and profit was mainly one of terminology. Reform enables employees to benefit from increased profitability, thus providing additional incentives to economic efficiency and rationality, which were not present in the 'command' mechanism.

One might query why it is necessary to have a separate profits tax at all, since the authorities already have three taxes at their disposal: turnover tax, wages tax, and capital charges, all of which influence enterprise profit. This seems a particularly pertinent question in the case of selectively decentralised socialism, where the authorities also control producer prices and retail prices, giving additional levers to affect profitability. When, then, a profits tax?

One possible answer may lie in Tinbergen's theory of economic policy (1970). Tinbergen sees the economic policy process as one of manipulating a set of policy instruments to achieve a set of given (quantitative) target variables. Optimality requires that there be the same number of policy instruments as there are (independent) policy targets. One may interpret this more broadly: if the tax system has a number of objectives, we need the same number of policy instruments as there are objectives. We have already outlined objectives for turnover tax (the level and structure of retail prices), for the wages tax (shadow pricing of labour) and for the capital charge (shadow pricing of capital). If we introduce a fourth objective, namely, determining enterprise residual net profit, then, assuming this is an independent objective, we need a fourth instrument. Thus the profits tax may be justified on the grounds of the multiple objectives of the system of business taxation.

If we turn from selective decentralisation to market socialism, the case for profits taxation becomes one of economic stabilisation. Since the central authorities relinquish central price controls in market socialism, as we have defined it in this book, they relinquish an instrument of economic stablisation policy. These direct controls can be replaced by profits taxation, which influences corporate net profits, and, ultimately, the growth of labour income in the economy. Profits tax has the further advantage that it can be levied at progressive rates, so providing some automatic stabilising properties of the tax system which can help to offset economic fluctuations.

In the economic theory of public finance, the economic effects of profits taxation, especially the incidence of the tax represent an area of controversy. Standard theory predicts that, so long as firms are profit maximising, a tax on pure profits from capital rests, in the short run, on the owners of the taxed capital. Profits are defined as the difference between total costs and total revenues. Since profits are a residual, a tax on profits does not affect the marginal conditions for profit maximisation, and thus the firm's price and output are unaffected by the tax, although owners' profits are reduced. This conclusion is modified somewhat when we recognise that accounting profits used for tax assessments differ somewhat from the pure profits of economic theory. Taxable profit usually includes some elements of firm's costs, notably, costs of dividend capital, which are not tax deductible, and certain non-deductible expenses (such as entertaining clients). Some of the profits tax falls on cost, and we would expect some forward shifting, with price rising, and output falling. In this case, part of the tax rests on the owners of taxed capital, part is shifted to consumers. (For details, see Harberger, 1962; or any standard textbook, such as Brown and Jackson, 1982, pp.402-413). The theory applies to firms, regardless of whether they are price takers or price makers, so the distinction between selectively decentralised socialism and market socialism does not matter here; when the central authorities control prices, State corporations must be assumed to act as price-takers.

Can this theory be applied to the socialist economy? It is possible to argue that in the socialist economy the difference between accounting profits and pure profits is somewhat narrower. In fact, provided we can make three assumptions, there would be no difference between pure and accounting profits in the socialist economy. These three assumptions are:

1. the socialist enterprise pays tax-deductible interest (or a capital charge) on all the capital it uses.
2. all expenses incurred by the socialist enterprise are tax deductible.
3. there are no differences between accounting and economic depreciation.

Provided taxable profits are equal to pure profits, a profits tax on the socialised enterprise would leave price and output unaffected in the short run. Moreover, if there is complete central control over investment, so that investment is completely unresponsive to market forces, this conclusion would apply in the long run as well. A profits tax would, in these circumstances, be completely non-distorting and hence would be the most 'efficient' tax for transferring control over profits from the enterprise to the central authorities.

One possible distorting effect must be noted however. In our model, incentives are profit-related, a profits tax can affect work effort. The effect is ambiguous however: the income effect tends to increase work effort, while the substitution effect acts to reduce effort and increase leisure taking. In this context, it should be noted that the tax on pure profits is a more effective way of regulating the incentives fund than the payroll tax is. Taxes on factor inputs raise costs and influence the supply curve, so they are shifted forwards and raise market price. Provided enterprises maximise pure profits, however, a profits tax rests on producers.

We have so far assumed that socialist enterprises are instructed to maximise profits and do, in fact do so. This is the basis of our theoretical predictions about tax incidence and resource allocation. But, since information is imperfect, neither central planners nor enterprise managers actually know what the maximum amount of profit would be. Lange (1976, p.88) argues that maximum profit could be found by trial and error. Even in principle, trial and error would not necessarily establish maximum profit. Cost and revenue curves may simply not be as 'well-behaved' as those in the textbooks. Leads and lags may prevent convergence on a stable equilibrium. Dynamic considerations, ever-changing technology and cost conditions, the fickleness of market demand, are all factors which may rule out the possibility of reaching maximum profit by trial and error.

One may argue, however, that the issue is not whether managers ever actually reach maximum profit, but whether they strive to do so. Do they prefer more profit to less? If the answer is yes, then managers will behave in the classic, profit-maximising way. Their response to external stimuli (such as a fall in demand or a change in the price of a competing product) will be the same as that predicted by the theory of profit maximisation. When incentives are profit-related, managers have a financial interest in making more profit. We might, therefore, expect them to behave as profit-maximisers, so that the efficiencies of profit-orientated business behaviour can be reaped by the socialist economy. Compared to the command mechanism, the profit-maximising manager in a reformed mechanism will use resources more efficiently: it is in his/her interests to make cost-reducing innovations, search for cheaper sources of supply, and to produce what customers want to buy. The waste and inefficiency generated by producing 'for the plan' are eliminated by producing 'for the market'. Inefficiencies arising from other sources may remain (such as those resulting from the monopolistic structure of State industry), but decentralisation can tackle the problem of the inefficiencies of the 'command' management of the socialist economy.

Yet we must surely consider the possibility that managers may not pursue the goal of profit maximisation. In the theory of the behaviour of 'capitalist' firms, it is argued by a wide range of theorists that managers of capitalist corporations do not single-mindedly pursue the goal of profit maximisation. Indeed, they may actually sacrifice profit to pursue other goals, such as sales, (see Baumol, 1967) or they may maximise an objective function in which there are a multiplicity of arguments, of which profits are only one. Profit may be traded off against other variables, in pursuit of the maximisation of overall managerial utility (see Williamson, 1970). Managers may simply seek an adequate level of profits: one which keeps shareholders happy, and keeps managers in a job: they 'satisfice', rather than'maximise'.(see Simons, 1961).

How likely is such non-profit maximising behaviour in market socialism? Satisficing behaviour seems particularly likely. Managers of socialised enterprises might simply make enough profit to make adequate bonuses, and keep superiors happy. The point about the 'adequate' level of bonus may be related to the shortages of desirable consumer goods which has been so typical of centrally planned economies; there is no point in making superhuman managerial efforts to improve bonuses, if the extra money cannot be spent. (Similar considerations may apply to profit-related incentives for workers; their work effort may also be blunted if their extra income cannot be turned into satisfying purchases). This implies that one of the considerations for successful implementation of market socialism is the maintenance of market equilibrium. In disequilibrium conditions, potential efficiency gains are lost.

Another possible reason for satisficing may be that managers believe in a kind of 'financial ratchet' principle - large profits this year may result in profits tax being changed next year to cream off excess profits. Keeping profits down to a 'safe' level may make life easier for managers in future.

Supposing satisficing, rather than maximising behaviour, is the rule, what are the implications for the incidence of a profits tax? It is usually argued that, where non-profit objectives are pursued, profit will be less than the maximum, so that firms can shift the tax forward to consumers. Certain researchers in this area have claimed that taxes are shifted forward by 100%, leaving the profit margin of the firm unaffected. (For a summary of these arguments, see Mieszkowski, 1972, and Break, 1974, pp.138-154). The question then arises how consumers react to higher prices. In normal conditions of market equilibrium, demand for products would fall, output would be reduced, and there would be a loss of profits, and an excess burden arising from the tax. Many researchers seem to argue, however, that forward shifting does not have these effects; the higher price is simply accepted by consumers. One can certainly accept this might be the case in conditions of excess demand for the product, or if the level of demand in the economy is generally rising. In the context of capitalist producers it is difficult to accept that firms normally operate in conditions of excess demand for their products. Permanent shortages of consumer goods might, however, be thought to be more common in socialist countries. In this case, forward shifting of a tax on profits (or any other tax, for that matter) might be potentially useful in mopping up excess demand.

TAXATION OF THE MARKET SECTOR

The Market sector survives, in socialist economies, as a residual sector consisting largely of self-employed businessmen. Although this is a peripheral sector, it is not insigniiicant. However, the scope of Market activities varies considerably among the socialist economies. Peasant agriculture survives to greater or lesser extent everywhere, but official policy towards other private sector activities varies. The Soviet Union tends to place tight restrictions on private sector activities, but other countries are more tolerant, even supportive on occasion. On the whole, private sector activities tend to be confined to the service sector, and to the literary and artistic field.

State policy towards the Market sector involves of the scope of Market activity, the balance between Planned and Market activity, and the appropriate fiscal and legal regime for Market sector producers. The role of the Market (private) sector in a socialist economy can be regarded in a variety of ways. One rather stereotyped view would be to regard the Market sector as some kind of unsocialist anachronism, a survival from the past, which will eventually wither away - helped along, perhaps, by punitive taxation, levied as a matter of State policy.

However, the view taken in this book is

that Plan, Market and Budget should be regarded as complementary allocative mechanisms (see Ch.1). The author's view is that planning need not and does not require abolition of the Market sector, and that the continued existence of a Market sector in a socialist economy is functional, and not just an accident.

In certain circumstances, the Market mechanism is a more efficient allocator of resources than the Plan; this follows from our arguments of Ch.1, based on Williamson (1975). However, though Williamson deals at length with the circumstances in which internal decision-making (i.e. the Plan sector) is more efficient than the Market, the reader is not given much guidance as to the conditions under which the Market is the more efficient solution to the allocation problem.

Galbraith (1975, especially Chs.5-8) offers more guidance, pointing out that organisational economies are unlikely to be significant where tasks are unstandardised and geographically dispersed, nor where there is an explicit demand for personal services, nor in certain literary or artistic activities. Furthermore, Galbraith argues, the personal incentives of self-employment give a strong motivation to both efficiency and independence. Thus, the personal reward for independent operation may well outweigh organisational economies as a factor in ensuring supplies of goods and services at low cost, in some, if not all, cases.

If the Market sector can contribute efficiently to national output, then taxation of Market activities must be based on efficiency considerations, as well as principles of equity and distributive justice. The classic efficient tax is land tax, in the form of a tax on pure rent. Land tax extracts economic rent ('unearned' income) and also encourages work effort and economic efficiency. Land tax has a pure income effect, which encourages work effort, but since the marginal tax rate on effort or its rewards is zero, there is no discouraging substitution effect. Socialist economies often tax agriculture differently to other forms of production, and a land tax has great efficiency advantages in agricultural taxation. Land tax can also be (roughly) related to the natural fertility and productivity of the soil; so that it becomes a tax on earning potential, introducing a certain element of distributive justice. The land tax can, in principle, satisfy criteria of both economic efficiency and (vertical) equity: it appears to be an 'optimal' tax.

Lump-sum taxes are known to be efficient, since they have no distorting effects on substitution at the margin, but, at the same time, lump-sum taxes are normally regressive (with respect to income) in their incidence, and are therefore considered inequitable. An element of equity could theoretically be introduced by taxing individuals on the ability to earn income (rather than on actual income). However most writers dismiss this solution as infeasible (e.g. Brown and Jackson, 1982, p.431). The case of agricultural land tax suggests a solution, but, of course, not all citizens working in the Market sector farm the land.

One possible solution comes from Poland, where the Market sector is relatively highly developed among artisans, shopkeepers, keepers of cafes and restaurants, taxi drivers and other services. These private sector suppliers would normally be liable to sales tax on their output, and income tax on their profits. However, in 1977 the authorities introduced arrangements whereby sales tax and income tax could be commuted into a single lump-sum payment of franchise tax, which removed the need to pay sales tax and income tax for a number of years. The tax was graded according to occupation, which can presumably be regarded as a rough proxy for potential earnings. A further refinement was that the franchise tax rose as the number of employees, if any.

As well as combining principles of equity and efficiency, the use of franchise tax implies some administrative economies. The taxpayer escapes the need to keep detailed accounts for tax purposes, so compliance costs are reduced. The tax authorities avoid the costs of annual assessment and collection of tax. Though the amount of franchise tax is reassessed every three years, the computation is very much simpler than that required for computing annual taxable profits. It would seem that many other tax authorities in the world might wish to copy such a tax, but there are disadvantages. Revenue yield is very inelastic, and defining occupations can be troublesome. The zero marginal tax rate creates an impression (correct) that income is untaxed, which can be a cause of resentment among fellow citizens; an especially difficult problem in socialist countries where the private sector may be a source of tension. However, franchise tax can also be used to overcome problems of tax evasion and failure of taxpayers to keep adequate records.

SUMMARY

This chapter has examined the role of taxes on capital and profits. The case for a tax on capital employed by socialised enterprise was discussed in terms of its desirable allocative effects. The case for taxing profits was examined, and it was argued that a suitably defined base for profits taxation would result in profits taxation being neutral in its effects on resource allocation; this could be useful where other taxes (on wages and capital) are being used precisely because their effects are non-neutral. A neutral profits tax would avoid distorting the effects of other taxes, but would allow the authorities to regulate residual enterprise profits and raise budgetary revenue. The taxation of the residual Market sector was discussed on the assumption that, even in a socialist economy, some Market allocation remains appropriate. The case for lump-sum franchise taxes was advocated on efficiency grounds.

REFERENCES

ANDERSON, E.E. (1983), 'Central Planning and Production Instabilities in Eastern Europe' Slavic Review Vol.42, No.2, pp.221-230

BAJGUSZ, J. (1977) 'The influence of budgetary instruments on State enterprises' (Polish) Finanse No.5, May, pp.17-26

BAJT, A. (1971) 'Investment Cycles in European Socialist Economies' Journal of Economic Literature Vol.9, pp.53-63

BAUMOL, W.J. (1967) Business Behaviour, Value and Growth rev. ed., Harcourt, Brace and World, New York

BIRMAN, I. (1981) Secret Incomes of the Soviet State Budget Martinus Nijhoff Publishers, The Hague, Boston and London

BREAK, G.F. (1974) 'The Incidence and Economic

Effects of Taxation' in A.S. Blinder et al. The Economics of Public Finance Brookings Institution, Washington D.C.

BROWN, C.V. and JACKSON, P.M. (1982) Public Sector Economics Martin Robertson, Oxford, 1982

FEDOROWICZ, Z. (1978) The Economic-Financial Mechanism for Steering Economic Units (Polish) State Economic Publishers, Warsaw

FELDSTEIN, M.S. (1972) 'The Social Time Preference Discount Rate in Cost-Benefit Analysis' in R Layard (ed.) Cost-Benefit Analysis Penguin, Harmondsworth, Middlesex

GALBRAITH, J.K. (1975) Economics and the Public Purpose Penguin, Harmondsworth, Middlesex

HARBERGER, A.C. (1962) 'The Incidence of the Corporation Income Tax' Journal of Political Economy Vol.70, pp.215-240

HARE, P.G. (1983) 'The Beginnings of Institutional Reform in Hungary' Soviet Studies Vol.35, pp.313-330

HARE, P.G. and WANLESS, P.T. (1981) 'Polish and Hungarian Economic Reforms: A Comparison' Soviet Studies Vol.32, pp.491-517

LANGE, O. (1976) 'On the Economic Theory of Socialism' in O. Lange and F.M. Tahlor 'On the Economic Theory of Socialism' reprinted Tata - McGraw Hill, New Delhi

LEPTIN, G. and MELTZER, M. (1978) Economic Reforms in East German Industry Oxford University Press

MIESZKOWSKI, P. (1969) 'Tax Incidence Theory' Journal of Economic Literature Vol.7, pp. 1103-1124

SIMON, H.A. (1961) Administrative Behaviour 2nd ed., Macmillan, New York

TINBERGEN, J. (1970) On the Theory of Economic Policy 5th printing, North-Holland Publishing Co., Amsterdam and London

WAKULSKA, M. (1975) 'Capital Charges on Fixed Assets in Industrial Pilot Units' (Polish) Finanse No. 8/9, August/September, pp.45-49

WILLIAMSON, O.E. (1970) Corporate Control and Business Behaviour Prentice-Hall, New York

WILLIAMSON, O.E. (1975) Markets and Hierarchies: Analysis and Anti-Trust Implications Free Press, New York

Chapter 8

CONCLUDING THOUGHTS AND DIRECTIONS FOR FUTURE RESEARCH

THE COMPLEXITY OF SOCIALIST TAX SYSTEMS

In this book, the question of taxation in the socialist economy has been explored by means of a simplified model, in which the State Budget is supported by four taxes: turnover tax, wages tax, capital charges, and profits tax. This was an expositional device, intended to make the analysis of socialist taxation more manageable. In practice, the taxation of real world socialist economies is much more complex than the four tax model suggests. This complexity has been mentioned several times in this book, especially in Chapter 4.

This real world complexity takes a variety of forms. Some of the taxes levied in socialist economies do not fit readily into the categories of the model. These include, for example, agricultural land tax, and taxes on personal income and wealth. In other cases, real world taxes can be fitted into the categories, but more than one tax can be put into each category. For example, sales taxation falls into the turnover tax category, but can take a variety of forms, and can also include taxes on foreign trade. Wages tax can include social security contributions, levied as payroll taxes, as well as the payroll taxes on the wage fund introduced in the course of economic reforms. The capital tax category could include real estate taxes, while profits tax could include taxes on the 'funds' formed from profits, as well as taxes on profits proper. Thus different forms of tax levied on the same or closely related tax bases contribute to the complexity of socialist taxation.

Furthermore, the types of taxes levied in socialist countries vary among countries and over time. In part this may represent different economic structures and fiscal traditions. The variations are also associated with the country's experience of attempting economic reform, and the type of reform envisaged. Though the approaches to economic reform have often been broadly similar, details have differed. There are certainly enough similarities to be able to talk about a model of socialist taxation, but, at the same time, the idiosyncracies of individual countries are a fact of life which must be faced.

In terms of future research on the taxation of socialist economies, real world complexity has a number of implications. Any approach adopted must be sufficiently flexible to incorporate a multiplicity of taxes, sufficiently flexible to incorporate real world diversity, but, at the same time, be general enough to apply to all centrally planned economies. This is a tall order, and the rest of the chapter is devoted to sketching out some possible areas of future research.

IDEAL CHARACTERISTICS OF FUTURE RESEARCH

Future research must take account of the special characteristics of the socialist economy, as well as the complexity of its tax system. These special characteristics can be summed up briefly. The socialist economy is centrally planned, and the means of production are owned collectively. Typically, the socialist economy is a resource-constrained economy; that is, it is in disequilibrium, caused by supply side constraints, so that the economy is in a condition of shortage, with persistent excess demand for goods and services. (Kornai, 1980, especially pp.1-16.)

What directions should future research take? One of the most pressing and interesting tasks is surely to develop methods of analysis which could examine the economic effects of the complex tax packages introduced in the course of economic reforms. Thus we require an analysis which can handle both the introduction of new taxes and the effects of changing several different tax rates at the same time. Ideally, it would also incorporate other aspects of tax reform, such as changes in the rules governing the computation of the tax base. Because of the special characteristics of the socialist economy, the analysis would have to be applicable in conditions of economic disequilibrium, and would have to relate the effects of taxation to changes in the supply side constraints on the economy.

Because such an approach clearly requires a high level of aggregation, one of the approaches used in this book, Williamson's 'markets versus hierarchies' approach (1975), is of limited use, since it is basically a theory of organisations, applicable to the discussion of institutional arrangements, but less useful in tax analysis.

RESEARCH BASED ON PUBLIC FINANCE THEORY

The requirements outlined above also pose some problems in applying the economic theory of public finance to the analysis of socialist taxation. Much of economic theory is concerned with the analysis of equilibrium. In the economic theory of public finance, a great deal of the analysis of tax changes is conducted in terms of the comparative statics of partial equilibrium at the microeconomic level, and allows for a change in only one tax rate at a time.

Although this approach looks somewhat unfruitful, the microeconomics of public finance do provide us with one potentially useful analytical device, namely, that of analysing tax changes on the assumption that total tax revenue is held constant. This is useful, since it allows the analyst to separate the effects of changes in tax rates from the macroeconomic effects of changes in the size of tax revenue, or of changes in the balance of the budget. (For more discussion, see standard texts such as Brown and Jackson, 1982 or Musgrave, 1959.)

The microeconomic analysis of tax changes, conducted on a constant revenue basis, can be complemented with macroeconomic theories of fiscal policy, which provide analyses of the effects of changes in tax revenue, and changes in budget balance. However, both at micro and macro level, the theory of public finance still suffers from the defect of equilibrium analysis. Moreover, the separation of micro and macro effects has been presented here as an advantage, but could also be regarded as a disadvantage, as artificially separating two types of effect which typically occur together. In the real world, tax changes usually alter both the rate of tax, and the amount of tax revenue. Nevertheless, it may be useful to separate the analytical treatment of micro and macro effects, provided the two approaches can be married up again at some point. Unfortunately, one of the defects of modern Western-style economics has been to keep microeconomics and macroeconomics rigidly separate, using quite different and incompatible approaches to explain behaviour at the two levels.

In spite of the limitations of public finance theory discussed so far, it is possible to obtain some general indication of directions for future research in each of our four taxation areas.

Applications to the four-tax model

Turnover tax, and related sales taxes, can be approached in terms of changing relative prices. An obvious item on the research agenda would be empirical investigation into the extent of forward shifting of such taxes in socialist economies, in conditions of administered pricing, and in market-determined prices.

Turnover tax could also be approached by means of its role in determining the general level and structure of consumer prices, with consequent effects upon the level and distribution of consumer incomes, and the level of demand in the consumer goods market, both in aggregate, and in individual product markets. One important area of enquiry is the question of how price-sensitive is consumer demand in conditions of shortage, with respect to both relative prices, and absolute prices. The extent to which price elasticity of demand is a function of shortage clearly influences the effectiveness of turnover tax as an instrument for securing market equilibrium. The effect of turnover tax on producer prices is also an item for further research, following the challenge to received wisdom offered by Drabek, 1979.

Another important question is the effect of turnover taxation on corporate profitability, clearly related to the need for research into tax shifting in socialist economies. With 100% forward shifting, turnover tax would not affect corporate profit margins, and would be ineffective as a regulator of corporate profitability. If shifting is less than 100%, however, then turnover tax may indeed influence profitability, though research would be needed to see if economic incidence reflected a similar pattern to legal incidence (which presumably indicates the central planners' intentions about the distribution of the tax burden).

Wage fund tax is a tax which is apparently of supply-side importance, through its effect on work effort and incentives. However, conventional public finance theory deals with the effect of taxation on personal incentives and individual work effort. Further developments in socialist wage taxation would require a theory of group motivation, and collective incentives - perhaps an approach based on organisational rather than conventional economic behaviour. Tax shifting may also, of course, be an issue here; if wages tax is shifted forward 100% in prices, it will have no effect on corporate profits and wage funds, as tax is simply recovered from customers. Questions of the perceptions of managers and workers may be relevant here. Do managers actually use the accounting or shadow prices of labour in making allocation decisions? Do workers actually feel that the tax system influences wage income? What effects do these perceptions have on allocative efficiency, and on industrial relations? Rapidly, we move from socialist taxation into labour market behaviour, into organisational behaviour, into corporate decision-making.

Questions of organisational behaviour and corporate decision-making also arise in connection with capital charges. How effective is the shadow-pricing function? How, if at all, do shadow prices enter the response function of managers of State corporations? Clearly, the most important decision-making area is that of investment decision-making, especially where decentralised investment at managerial discretion occurs on any scale. Studies of decentralised investment decisions in a socialist context offer considerable potential.

Corporate decisions, of course, do not just cover labour matters and capital investment. The setting of producer prices whether determined at central planning ('Head Office') level, or at corporate level, is another area for research, especially how, and to what extent, taxes on factors are incorporated into cost-plus prices.

Profits tax is another tax which could potentially effect decision-making. Chapter 7 argued that profits tax might be a neutral tax, an obviously interesting and attractive area. However, in Chapter 7, profits tax was assumed to have no effect on investment plans, but, where decentralised, discretionary investment is allowed, profits tax might affect investment through its effect on corporate retained profits and cash flows.

Overall, partial equilibrium analysis suggests some research topics which can advance the approach outlined in this book, especially in empirical research about the allocative impact of socialist taxation. However, partial equilibrium analysis may be of limited applicability to a socialist, resource-constrained economy, as it is both partial in nature, and concerned with equilibrium.

DIRECTIONS FOR FURTHER WORK: GENERAL EQUILIBRIUM ANALYSIS AND DISEQUILIBRIUM THEORY

One obvious way of overcoming problems of the limited applicability of partial equilibrium analysis would be to develop a general equilibrium approach to the analysis of socialist taxation. However, this is a relatively underdeveloped area of public finance theory. Nevertheless, this is an area already incorporated, albeit briefly into standard text books. Brown and Jackson outline three possible approaches(1983,Ch.12).

The most well developed in the Harberger model, originally developed in connection with the incidence of corporation tax. It is a severely limited model, based on a two sector economy, and capable of handling only one tax at a time. It is thus not a suitable framework for handling the kind of tax packages included in economic reforms. Moreover, attempts by Ratti and Shome (1977) to generalise the Harberger model to three sectors, appear to show that Harberger's results do not hold in the more general case.

A more promising approach might be the approach of Whalley and Shoven (1973) who have developed an algorithm which can handle the effects of tax packages. Based on extremely sophisticated mathematical techniques, it poses heavy information requirements; though it is possible that a socialist State might find it easier to collect information than a capitalist one, it is still not clear that all the information required by the algorithm could be collected at a reasonable cost and in a reasonable time. This approach also has the defect that it is not well suited to handling all the possible effects of tax changes - for example, the work/leisure choice is not well specified.

Finally, Brown and Jackson claim that input-output analysis could be used as a method of general equilibrium analysis, provided the assumption of fixed coefficients holds. Since we normally assume that taxes do alter economic behaviour, this approach seems difficult to justify. In the case of a socialist economy, an assumption of fixed coefficients might be justified in the short-run, or the case of the 'command' economy model, but is more difficult to justify after economic reforms have been introduced, especially if more scope is allowed for managerial discretion and market forces.

However, although general equilibrium theory has made some progress in public finance, there remains the consideration that we have already stated that future work in the theory of socialist taxation must be based on a dis-equilibrium approach. Two possible approaches may be considered - that outlined by Barro and Grossman in their path breaking work of 1976, and the approach developed specifically for socialist economies by Kornai, 1982 - an approach Kornai has called "the economics of shortage."

Barro and Grossman have argued that both conventional "classical" and "Keynesian" macroeconomics are at fault in simply not recognising that an economy in macroeconomic disequilibrium behaves differently to an economy in equilibrium at full employment - which can be the only 'true' equilibrium, characterised by absence of excess demand or supply. Barro and Grossman's argument is that an economy in macro disequilibrium is characterised by constraints which prevent it reaching full employment - but the very constraints which are present in disequilibrium, but not in equilibrium, these constraints alter the behaviour of economic actors. Put simply, suppose that, in equilibrium, the response Y occurs in response to an economic stimulus X. Barro and Grossman's argument is that, in disequilibrium, economic actors are faced with a number of constraints, and, as a result, the response to stimulus X is now Z, rather than the equilibrium response Y. In terms of a macroeconomic model, the constraints enter the behavioural equations, creating new ones, in line with the altered responses. In Kornai's terms, at the microeconomic level, the response function of decision makers is altered (see p.16).

As an example of how behaviour is altered by disequilibrium constraints, Barro and Grossman (p.85) argue that, as an economy characterised by excess demand, employment and output may actually be reduced <u>below</u> the full employment level; in other words, excess demand may cause unemployment. Such unemployment would be voluntary, arising because individuals, frustrated by shortages of goods in their attempts to achieve consumption plans, reduce their effective supply of labour. They attempt to achieve their planned utility level by consuming more leisure, in place of the goods they cannot purchase. This could give rise to the situation where a fiscal stimulus to output and work effort actually resulted in a rise in voluntary unemployment - a result at variance with conventional macroeconomic predictions.

Barro and Grossman's approach has been applied to centrally planned economics in order to study inflationary pressure - for example, by Howard (1976) and Portes and Winter (1980) - but not, so far, in order to study taxation. However, the approach is one which offers a general framework, integrates micro and macroeconomics, and incorporates disequilibrium phenomena.

On the other hand, Kornai's approach is specifically concerned with disequilibrium in the socialist economy, which he sees as operating in conditions of chronic shortage, where resource constraints are more important than demand constraints as determinants of output. In such an atmosphere, price signals may be less important in determining behaviour than resource constraints and non-price signals, in the form of quantity adjustments. Kornai (1980, pp.476-479) takes issue with the Barro-Grossman approach, arguing that in their model, shortage implies that consumers simply build up excess money balances. Kornai argues that shortage is not necessarily characterised by macroeconomic disequilibrium and excess money balances. Rather, it may be a case of disequilibrium at the microeconomic level, which is disguised at the macroeconomic level by the phenomena of forced substitution and forced spending. Forced substitution occurs when consumers turn to a less preferred substitute - for example, when a housewife goes out to buy veal, finds none in the shops, and comes home with a chicken. Forced spending occurs when the consumer buys some other product, rather than holding money balances; for example, the housewife, finding no meat in the shops, buys light bulbs or a new dress instead. Such behaviour may be motivated by impatience ("let's buy something, at any rate") or by "consumer manoeuvring" ("we'll need light bulbs anyway, and they might not be there when we do") or by fear of inflation ("they'll be more expensive soon"). In Kornai's view, shortage is a microeconomic phenomenon, arising because the constraints of the planning system do not allow the mix of output to respond to consumer demand.

In a resource constrained system, the tax system's influence may well operate through changes in budget constraints, rather than through price signals. Tax analysis would be conducted in terms of how budget constraints of consumers and producers were affected, in what direction, and how shortage was affected, both in aggregate and in individual product markets. This would suggest an approach radically different to that found in conventional public finance theory, and different to the approach generally used in this book (though the relevance of shortage has occasionally been noted; on p.35, and p.119, for example, and earlier in this chapter).

So far, there has been little attempt to integrate the question of taxation into "the economics of shortage." In Kornai's book of that name (1980), taxation is hardly mentioned, and the State Budget is, with one exception, mentioned only in passing. The exception is a short passage on the influence of a deficit or surplus in the State Budget upon the extent of shortage in the economy. Kornai argues that both the experience of the socialist economy, and theoretical reasoning, suggest that there is no simple relationship between the balance of the State Budget and the extent of shortage (pp.558-560). Experience suggests that sometimes socialist economies with a budget surplus experience an intensification of shortage, in other cases, a budget deficit is accompanied by a relaxation of shortage. Kornai stresses that the influence of the balance of the State Budget upon shortage depends on the balance of income and expenditure in other sectors of the economy. An increase in the State Budget deficit which offsets a rise in the surplus of the household sector is not likely to intensify excess demand, while if the rise in surplus of the household sector exceeds the rise in the deficit of the State Budget, excess demand may diminish and shortage may become less marked. To some extent such comments echo remarks made earlier in this book, pp.66,68.

Kornai is also very concerned with the effect of the State Budget upon how 'hard' or 'soft' are the budget constraints of other economic units, but looks at this only in terms of subsidies paid to those units, especially socialised enterprises. Yet work on 'tax expenditures' in the United States and in Britain suggests that reducing taxes may be a means of hidden or disguised subsidy, while the influence of taxation on after-tax profits, and on incentive funds, must surely be an issue in the case of socialised enterprises. If the 'economies of shortage' is to provide a vehicle for further work on socialist taxation, it must be explicitly incorporated into the analysis. On balance, Kornai's work seems more appropriate than Barro and Grossman's, since Kornai's work is specifically geared to the special conditions of the socialist economy. It is here, perhaps, that further developments in the theory of socialist taxation can occur. The present book has taken the first steps in developing a theory of socialist taxation, but many more steps remain.

REFERENCES

BARRO, R.J. and GROSSMAN, H.I. (1976) Money, Employment and Inflation, Cambridge University Press

BROWN, C.V. and JACKSON, P.M. (1982) Public Sector Economics 2nd ed., Martin Robertson, Oxford

DRABEK, Z. (1979) 'Estimation and Analysis of Turnover Tax in Centrally Planned Economies with Special Reference to Czechoslovakia' Public Finance Vol.34, pp.196-224

HOWARD, D.H. (1976) 'The Disequilibrium Model in a Controlled Economy. An Empirical Test of the Barro-Grossman Model' American Economic Review, Vol.66, pp.871-879

KORNAI, J. (1980) Economics of Shortage North Holland Publishing Co., Amsterdam, New York and London

MUSGRAVE, R.A. (1959) The Theory of Public Finance McGraw-Hill, Kogakusha International Student Edition, Tokyo

PORTES, R. and WINTER, D. (1980) 'Disequilibrium Estimates for Consumption Goods Markets in Centrally Planned Economies' Review of Economic Studies Vol.47, pp.137-159

RATTI, R.A. and SHOME, P. (1977) 'The Incidence of the Corporation Tax: a Long-Run Specific Factor Model' Southern Economic Journal Vol.44, pp.85-99

SHOVEN, J. and WHALLEY, J. (1973) 'General Equilibrium with Taxes: A Computational Procedure and an Existence Proof 'Review of Economic Studies Vol.40, pp.465-489

WILLIAMSON, O.E. (1975) Markets vs Hierarchies: Analysis and Anti-Trust Implications

Directions for Future Research

Free Press, New York

INDEX

For Product Safety Concerns and Information please contact our
EU representative GPSR@taylorandfrancis.com Taylor & Francis
Verlag GmbH, Kaufingerstraße 24, 80331 München, Germany